LIVING **LIFE** IN **COLOR** AGAIN

NOTES FROM A HOMICIDE SURVIVOR

A Grief Memoir with Journal Prompts

KIMBERLY CHRISTOPHER

For more information, contact: kimberlyvchristopher@gmail.com

First print edition May, 2024
Revised August 2024

Cover art by Eugene Bennett and Kimberly V. Christopher
Edited by Mozelle Jordan
Book design by Veronica Scott

ISBN 979-8-218-40810-7 (paperback)

For my first friend, Keith.

Dear Brother

Thought we had more time

Taken from us—it's not fair

Nephew bears your name

Contents

Introduction

Today is my brother Keith's birthday. If he were alive, he would have been forty-nine years old. Today is also the first time that I am sitting down to write about how his tragic death has affected me and how I learned, and am still learning, to unpack my grief.

Months ago, I began to jot down ideas for the book I would inevitably write and even created voice notes to keep chapter ideas fresh. Eventually, I was able to create a rough outline and felt pleased about the direction in which the book was moving. But when it finally came time to make those ideas come to life through words, I found it difficult to actually sit and write. Maybe I wanted to avoid the tidal wave of emotion that I knew would consume me. Maybe I wanted to avoid the anxiety and anger that still found me more than two decades after my brother's life was taken. Either way, there had been something deeply rooted within me for over twenty years that made me ignore the calling of writing *Living Life in Color Again*. As the years passed, it became harder to suppress my emotions.

Only once before have I felt this much reluctance to complete a task—when my mother passed away nine years ago. I needed to provide the memorial mason a mock-up of my desired customizations for the companion headstone to represent the side-by-side graves of her and my brother. I sat at my laptop for a few moments trying to draft a picture but then jumped up to refill my water cup, get a snack, or do anything that would help me procrastinate just a little bit longer. After I ran out of things to keep me preoccupied, I meandered slowly back to my chair. Something that should have taken me twenty minutes to finish took me weeks to do. The tension between my desire to complete that task and my instinct to avoid the pain was thick.

But since today is Keith's birthday, writing doesn't feel like a chore. Instead, it feels like a way to honor my first friend, my brother, who was taken from us in an act of senseless gun violence, an event that has become all too common in the United States. My journey through grief has been arduous, painful, and non-linear. Let me correct that; my journey through grief IS arduous, painful, and non-linear. Even after more than two decades, my grieving has not ended. There are simply the early years of grieving, and now, the later years.

During my early years of grief, the pain of my brother's homicide was raw and intense. I did not have the words to express my thoughts and feelings and was embarrassed that I cried so much. I felt fragile and sensitive, so I retreated, finding it best to stay in the comfort of my solitude. I thought this was to protect myself, but I was only forcing myself to battle grief alone. I had neither sought the help of a trauma-informed therapist nor a community of people who could relate to my experience, and I lacked the wisdom to appreciate the value of having both. Two dear friends and their families were as supportive as they could be, for which I was thankful–especially in the absence of my extended family members' support. My mom tried to be there for me, but I knew that she had a lot of healing to do herself. So, I did the best that I could with what I had, which were outdated and unrealistic expectations of how I should behave based on mainstream beliefs about what grief and healing should look like. The expectations that I should feel better and move on by a certain timeframe created noise that has lingered with me ever since. I can't figure out how to silence that noise, either. The would have beens, should have beens, and could have beens follow me. With time, they have only grown louder. My mind has failed to make sense of why someone would commit such a heinous crime. This question and this wound wrapped around my pre-existing scars, blocking light for many decades and rendering bleak the possibility of healing and living fully.

After years of living in this darkened version of life, I finally started to dig into the painful effects of my brother's murder and felt ready to look at other parts of myself that needed healing as well. It is more accurate to say that I could no longer ignore the other parts of myself that needed healing. An invitation to speak with the Pennsylvania Board of Parole about this loss' effect on me was my momentum for deep self-reflection. After months of reflection, I discovered the truth that my brother's homicide had been affecting me in both obvious and nuanced ways. I became curious about other breakthroughs awaiting me. I began to examine family history, dynamics, and patterns to understand their impact. For example, why did I wait so long to center my own healing?

Homicide is a heavy topic. It's not brunch conversation, and believe me, I learned that the hard way. Throughout the years, few family members and friends volunteered to hear my complex and depressing thoughts and feelings, which I find odd considering the popularity of film and television programs that center around murder. People tune in by the millions to watch fictional shows, documentaries, and autobiographies about homicidal maniacs. Yet, in my experience, the appetite seems low for bi-directional sharing of people's real-time experiences surrounding the loss of a murdered loved one. However, heavy or not, I have had no option but to always carry the weight of the topic with me. The knowledge that someone took the life of a person you love is not a thought that is ever forgotten.

My grief journey has been full of surprises, challenges, and contradictions. This twenty-five-year-old wound is like a scar that appears fully healed, yet remains tender to the touch. As I have moved through various stages and experiences in life, the pain has expanded and contracted, but no matter what, has always followed me like a shadow. It has made time pass excruciatingly slowly, yet I am shocked at how quickly the years have flown.

Two decades after my brother's murder, I realized how transformative this loss had been. My brother's death created a partition, marking the end of the years of my life that were effortlessly bright and full of color and beginning the years that felt lackluster and sad. And now, I am at another pivotal moment in my life; I was twenty-three when my brother was murdered, and pretty soon, I will have spent more time on this Earth without my brother than I have with him. This realization served as a personal inflection point, signaling a shift toward embracing life with a lightness and clarity that I have not felt in a long time. If this is in fact the start of a new chapter, I would like to spend it supporting other homicide survivors along their respective healing journeys.

While preparing for the fourth and final presentation to the Parole Board panel in 2022, I had a flashback to an episode of a sitcom. The producers of the show used monochrome film to represent an inflection point in a character's life; the film or TV show began in color, and then eventually, the color faded as a result of deep disappointment, trauma, and loss. The colors began to fade from my life in 1999, but I am pleased to say that the colors are making a triumphant return.

As a trauma survivor, I felt as if society was encouraging me to rush through the healing process. During my early years of grief, clergy members and co-workers seemed shocked that I had not gotten over my brother's death. I will never get over my brother's murder. I should not be expected to. It is insulting, unfair, and unhealthy to believe that homicide survivors can and should simply 'get over it.' The pain will remain with me for as long as I live. Consequently, I have chosen to stop running away from my grief and instead, develop a relationship with my grief–to engage with and meet it head-on, even when everything within me says to run away. I've learned that if not faced, the grief will control my life and continue to influence my decisions.

In *Living Life in Color Again: Notes from a Homicide Survivor*, I share my experiences with grief following my brother's homicide. I reference interactions with victim advocates and religious leaders, relatives, co-workers, friends, and strangers and examine the support and compassion extended by each. Some interactions were helpful; others were damaging. In some cases, I choose not to assume benign intent. I examine neither someone's "will" nor "skill" to be supportive. I focus on the impact of their actions, not the intent, because the former creates indelible impressions. The damaging conversations that I explore illustrate the importance of belonging to a community of others with similar lived experiences who can help you navigate those situations.

In my twenty-second year of grief, the advocate with whom I partnered during the Parole Board preparation process introduced me to a Philadelphia-based support group for homicide survivors. The members of this support group encourage each other, provide kind words during calls and group text messages, and share moments of laughter. The group gives a judgment-free space to express difficult and heavy emotions and a soft place to land after tougher moments. Through this group, I came to learn that circumstances surrounding the loss of our loved ones may heavily influence our grief journeys. People within the same bereaved family may even grieve differently. Therefore, I am healing within my context, one that reflects my familial, spiritual, social, and environmental dimensions, and I have given myself the grace to do so. As such, I have become the expert in my healing, and I encourage you to become the expert in yours.

With journal prompts and openness, this book is part workbook, part autobiography. I encourage you to make the most of the prompts, whether jotting your answers in the book or simply dedicating some time to think about them, as I have discovered a lot of myself within them. Perhaps something will resonate, offer a different perspective, or provide language, comfort, inspiration, or serve as an invitation for you to either create or revise your path toward healing. For starters, answering the following question led me to have extraordinary breakthroughs: What continuing effects have my brother's murder had on me? Articulating a reply required me to revisit the past and trudge through murky memories and experiences that I had avoided for years.

What worked for me may not work for you, and what was true for me may not be for you. My only hope is that my words and these pages guide you in finding your truth, allowing you to live life in color again.

PART I

A Cold Winter

CHAPTER ONE

The Monday That Changed Everything

Growing up, I hated the first month of the Gregorian calendar. In the Northern Hemisphere, January coincides with the middle of winter, which means frigid temperatures, bone-chilling wind, shorter days, and longer nights. As a summer baby who loves to feel the warmth of the sun's rays, I abhor everything that accompanies winter. Unlike its neighboring months, January also feels devoid of celebration. It lacks December's festive lights and spirit of peace and goodwill and February's commercial romance with the pops of pink and red. January was just ... there—delightfully doling out harshness in generous amounts. So, when I received word in late January that my brother was murdered, I had even more reason to loathe that month.

Nighttime.

Darkness.

Death.

On the last Monday of the month, I was eating lunch at my work desk and, as I regularly did, I called home to check my answering machine. There were rarely new messages waiting for me, but on that day, I heard my mom's voice—quiet and quivering—asking me to call her. I knew something was terribly wrong. I hung up and immediately called her house phone, but no one answered. In addition to living seven hours away and not being able to stop by her house, the year was 1999, and cell phones were not yet ubiquitous. There wasn't an option to call her mobile number, send her a text, or track her location using an app. All I could do was wait. In the anguish of waiting, my imagination and worry went into overdrive. Did something happen to someone I know?

I thought about our longtime family friend, whom we affectionately called Mr. Joe. Keith and I had known him since we were twelve and eleven years old, respectively, and would either see or speak to him multiple times each week. Mr. Joe had recently fallen down the basement stairs of his corner store. After hearing Ma's message, I began to think the worst. I called to check in on him and was relieved to learn that he was resting and doing well—albeit nursing a couple of bruised ribs. The relief quickly returned to worry as I remembered the sadness in my mom's voice. I called Ma's house again, and still, no answer. Then I wondered, "Why isn't Keith answering? He should be home." My brother lived at home and worked the third shift. Keith had never been a heavy sleeper, so hearing the phone ring multiple times around noon should have awakened him.

I panicked. Something wasn't right. I thought about whom to call next. Most of my mother's family lived in South Carolina, and for as long as I could remember, Ma and her siblings talked for hours on Sundays. If anyone knew what was going on, I knew that it would be Ma's sister. I called my aunt's house, and my cousin answered. "Hey, this is Kim..." I said. My cousin was silent, and I heard muffled voices. I tried again. "Hello? Hello?"

My cousin had given the receiver to her mom, my aunt, who delivered the news that changed my life. "Keith got killed."

A co-worker later told me that she heard a loud wail from my side of the hall. "It sounded like a wounded animal was back there," she said. I remember feeling like I had been kicked in the gut while doubling over, covering my stomach with my hand. I needed to talk to Ma. I ended the call with my aunt, and I walked down the hall to notify someone about my early departure due to an emergency.

One of the directors was eating lunch in her office, so without any small talk, I told her, "I just learned that my brother was killed. I need to go home and figure out what to do next."

"Oh, my God! Don't worry about work. Just call me once you've determined your next steps." With that, she shooed me out the door.

I grabbed my keys and purse from my desk drawer and headed for the elevator. I managed to drive myself to my apartment without incident, despite having cried the entire way there.

The spacious three-bedroom apartment was quiet, telling me that neither of my roommates were home. I tried to distract myself by staying busy with chores, which should have been easy to do; my roommates and I were moving into our own respective places soon, so packing boxes were everywhere, and there was a lot left to tackle. I resumed packing my room to avoid picking up the phone that rested on the table next to my bed and calling someone—anyone—who had some information about what was happening. But the more I tried not to fixate on using the phone, the more I found myself inching toward the receiver to call Ma's house.

I needed to get out of the apartment and away from the phone. I was low on packaging tape so that provided a good reason for an excursion. I changed clothes, put on a baseball hat, pulled it low onto my face to hide my eyes, and went to the store.

At the register, the cashier greeted me with a sincere, "How are you?"

Should I tell her that my stomach is in knots because I just found out that my brother is dead? Of course not. With a nod of affirmation, I lied to the kind cashier while wiping tears from the corners of my eyes. By the end of our exchange, I'm certain that my body language provided the real answer to her question. Nonetheless, with packaging tape in hand, I got in my car and drove back to my apartment.

I returned home and ran to my bedroom, anxious to check my answering machine. There were no new messages. I needed to talk to Ma. What was she doing? Did she need me? Within seconds of walking through the door, I called her house repeatedly, but no one answered.

Close to two hours later, she finally called me back, and though I had been praying for her to say my aunt had made a horrible mistake, she could only confirm the unspeakable. Through freshly fallen tears, I asked, "What do you need me to do? Go to Philadelphia and help you there, or go to South Carolina to help prepare for the funeral?" I was certain that she would want him to be buried in her home state and expected that, at some point, we'd all be going to South Carolina.

"If you could go to South Carolina to prepare for the funeral, I'll meet you there in a few days," she instructed.

CHAPTER TWO

The "Setting Up"

Given the time of day, a four-hour road trip from my apartment in North Carolina would have put me in South Carolina after dark, so I planned to leave the next morning. I spent the rest of "the Monday that changed my life" doing laundry, auditing my funeral attire, and packing enough clothes for a week. As my director requested, I also called to notify her of my travel plans and the number of days that I would be missing work. She expressed an interest in calling later to check in, so I gave my director the best contact number for me. By early evening, and after having gotten many more details figured out, I had calmed down—enough to leave the solitude of my room and engage with my roommates. I had left my bedroom door closed the entire afternoon. Before emerging from my room, I increased the volume of my landline phone's ringer to the maximum and left my bedroom door open so that I could hear any incoming calls.

I found my roommates sitting in the living room, so I joined them on the couch and matter-of-factly told them about Keith's death. If I could have left town without sharing the news, I would have done so, but my sudden absence—especially for seven days—would worry them. It was difficult to say the words *my brother was murdered* for the second time that day, but even so, one of them was surprised at my composed demeanor, noting that she would have been inconsolable had she received such news about her sibling. I was overwhelmed with emotion—too much to expel in one massive expression, but I knew within hours, my composed demeanor would unravel. And sure enough, it did.

The next day, I fueled up for the drive to my uncle's house for what South Carolinians call the "setting up"—a term used as both noun and verb. It describes the central location where bereaved family members converge to make funeral preparations and to receive well-wishers and expressions of support. After I contacted family members who were in that area and let them know of my plans, my uncle asked a few of my cousins to meet me at the North Carolina / South Carolina border so that I wouldn't have to drive the entire trip alone. I appreciated that so much. I wouldn't have thought to ask for the company.

As promised, Ma handled a few things with local entities in Philadelphia and arrived in the small town in South Carolina a couple of days after me. To say that was not the best circumstance for a reunion would be an understatement. We didn't have a lot of private time to talk when she arrived, so I could only hug her. I don't even think I asked how she was doing because I knew the answer.

Almost an hour after her arrival, Ma and I were able to sit together quietly in the dining room, at which time she provided me with a little more information: Keith was murdered early Saturday morning, and although the police immediately apprehended the two people responsible, they were unable to make an identification of Keith for two days because Keith was not carrying an ID, which is why it took them so long to notify her. After hearing the recount, we then quickly pivoted to funeral planning and focused on the details left to iron out. Even though it was the reason I went straight to South Carolina, I was not heavily involved in the funeral planning; I know Ma was grateful I was there, but I'm sure she tried to shield me from the stress of it all. While I stayed at my uncle's house, which was a veritable hotbed of social activity on any regular day, Ma opted to stay with her sister for what likely offered a quieter experience—and perhaps more amenable to managing grief while planning the funeral of her firstborn.

Since my uncle volunteered his home for the "setting up," for the next seven days, visitors were everywhere—inside and outside—offering support in the best ways they could. Not every moment of every day leading up to the funeral was heavy and tear-filled, as some would find out. Homemade biscuits, red velvet cakes, and baked macaroni and cheese found their way to the kitchen, enjoyed by all who visited. There were people in the den watching TV. Others throughout the house were having unrelated conversations.

Funeral and burial planning were time-sensitive tasks that required immediate decisions, and thanks to collaborative efforts between key family members and funeral home staff, some preliminary decisions were made while Ma was still in Philadelphia. However, a handful of decisions remained pending until Ma arrived in South Carolina. The morning after Ma's arrival, accompanied by a group of family members, we somberly drove into town to meet with the director of the quaint, family-owned funeral home to discuss the order of service and to view the body. We parked in the yard and quietly walked to the main entrance. It was then that I noticed a small marquee in the front yard that listed my brother's name: Mr. Keith Green. My stomach was in knots. I whispered something to myself and shook my head from left to right as if attempting to wipe that image from my memory. I could not believe any of it; it did not feel real. But what I was about to see inside the funeral home would ground that concept into a grim, undeniable reality. Nothing had prepared me to see my brother in a casket two months shy of his twenty-fifth birthday.

Later that day, as promised, the director from work called my uncle's house to check in with me. I struggled to hear her over multiple conversations happening in the background and as I began to chat with her, I could detect some surprise in her voice as she heard sounds of laughter drifting in from behind me. It didn't occur to me what outsiders may think of our grieving process, but I did appreciate her gesture in calling to see how I was doing.

There were much-needed moments of levity during the "setting up." While having the company of others was comforting, the consistent stream of people did not allow me the solitude I so desperately needed to process my thoughts and cry. But the beauty of living in the country is that family is never far away. Just yards from my uncle's house lived his sister-in-law. She had always been kind to me, and her home was peaceful. On the fourth day, my social battery was officially nonexistent, so I ran across the ditch to her house, knocked on her door, and accepted her invitation as she invited me in. She offered her condolences and asked how I was doing. And even though I didn't have the words with which to respond, I had plenty of tears. We talked as I cried non-stop for what felt like twenty minutes, and I was thankful she held space for me to do that. This Southern tradition—or maybe a South Carolina tradition—holds its grievers close, so I knew, at some point, people would be looking for me, so I reluctantly left the quiet moment with my uncle's sister-in-law to return to my uncle's house. But for a few minutes on that cold night in January, I needed to rebel against it and carve out a quiet place to cry.

There was one detail about that week that I found incredibly odd: the church and minister that hosted the funeral. I didn't press Ma for the specifics regarding any funeral arrangements, as I thought asking questions would only add to her stress, so I stayed in the dark regarding most of the arrangement details. Since the death of one of Ma's sisters a year prior, I had become a frequent visitor to this small South Carolina town. I attended church with my uncle and cousins, standing virtually every time to be recognized as a visitor. I had exchanged pleasantries with the pastor once or twice. My uncle and his family had been members of this church for years. So, naturally, I assumed that this church would host the funeral and that the pastor would be the one to eulogize my brother.

I was wrong.

It was not until after the funeral that I learned why he didn't: the pastor refused to host my brother's funeral because, based only on the fact that my brother's death was a homicide, the pastor concluded that Keith must have been involved with either drugs or a gang. With no supporting evidence, a minister decided that my brother was guilty of a crime and, consequently, not worth his time. And even if that were true, why did it matter? Do the details surrounding his death determine how one should respond to the bereaved family? What happened in Philadelphia was not as important as what my family and I needed at that moment. Some say a funeral should provide support and comfort for the ones left behind, in addition to remembering and honoring the dead. This pastor refused to honor my brother's memory and exiled Ma and me, almost as if Ma and I were "guilty by association." This was a terrible way to be treated. Instead of showing my mother the kindness and compassion she deserved, a self-professed servant of God told a grieving mother to find another church, since, in his opinion, her son must have been involved in suspicious activity that caused his untimely demise. Disappointed and disgusted best describe my feelings about that insult.

This experience taught me a valuable lesson: not every person who occupies a position or carries a title will provide emotional safety and compassion. The pastor wouldn't be the only one to have this perspective, either. Some of my experiences during the first couple of years of grief set the stage for the years to follow, introducing me to the themes and feelings that would recur throughout life—victim-blaming, selective empathy, and self-centered curiosity about the details surrounding my brother's death while expressing little concern for my well-being, and the importance of advocating for my wellness. Instead of reacting to me as if I had experienced trauma, during the years following Keith's death, many people fixated on the salacious details of the crime before deciding whether the context warranted either condolences or judgment. Even with the lesson learned, unintentionally, I had internalized those early instances of victim-blaming. I began to feel shame about this trauma and piled it onto my childhood story, which matched the narrative often seen in media: an inner-city youth from a broken home, raised by a stressed, depressed, and disillusioned single mother, who received little support from an abusive, alcoholic man who had fathered multiple children with multiple women. In retrospect, that kind of punitive self-shaming was unfair, unwarranted, and unproductive.

After the funeral, I told Ma that I would visit her in Philadelphia very soon, but first, I needed to return home to check in with my employer, vacate my current apartment, move into my new apartment, and refresh my clothing. So, a few days after the funeral, I returned to North Carolina and attempted to resume normal life activities.

CHAPTER THREE

The Quests for Justice and Normalcy

That first year was surreal. In retrospect, it felt like I was having an out-of-body experience, detached from everything and disconnected from everyone. I was like a spinning top, fueled by a fight or flight response that would not subside. I was successful at fulfilling the duties required of a human functioning in the natural world. I wore a mask and pretended that my life was not in shambles, compartmentalizing the pain of having watched my brother's coffin interred into the ground weeks prior. During work, I did my job and tried to maintain an upbeat demeanor. I was even praised by a co-worker for having returned to work so quickly after my brother's death, who muttered some gibberish about it being good to "get back in the saddle" on my first day back in the office. But what my co-workers didn't see is that, when it was necessary, I wept quietly at my desk or made several trips to the bathroom to have a proper cry in a bathroom stall.

For most of the first year, I cried multiple times every day: while in the shower, while driving to work, while driving home, and while shopping at the market. I went to the gym and occasionally cried as I ran laps and continued at home while sitting on the couch watching TV. The happy face I was able to muster up in between the tears was short-lived as I did not have the energy to sustain the façade.

During the last quarter of 1998, just a few months before my brother's passing, I had decided to pay kindness forward and applied to be part of the local chapter of the Big Brother / Big Sister Program. The program was established to foster one-on-one mentoring friendships between adult volunteers and children ages five through young adulthood who came from communities facing hardships. I completed the application process to become a Big Sister, and shortly after, I was told that I had been accepted. I was so excited. I finished orientation before the end of the year and looked forward to starting 1999 on a positive note.

But, as timing would have it, my brother passed unexpectedly, and only two months after the funeral, I was paired with my "Little Sister." Per the program's requirements, my Little Sister and I spent three to four hours together every week doing everyday activities like seeing a movie, completing homework, playing games, or going out to eat. Mental preparation was essential for those few hours a week. To create the best experience for a bright and energetic nine-year-old, I compartmentalized my feelings about losing my brother.

Occasionally, I met with the program sponsor to discuss how things were going with my Little Sister. During one of our meetings, I mentioned to her that I would need to go to Philadelphia a few times in the near future. She innocently assumed that I was traveling for fun, but when I told her about my brother's recent murder and that the trips to Philadelphia were for family visits, she was shocked and expressed the typical condolences. Nonetheless, she approved my time away and assured me that it wouldn't jeopardize my time in the program.

I continued to meet with my Little Sister weekly, but by August, I could no longer do it; my motor had run out. The emotional and mental investment required to feign wellness was too great, and I felt that withdrawing from the program was best. Although it was usually my program sponsor who initiated our meetings, this time, it was me who invited her to lunch at a casual restaurant so I could discuss something with her. The conversation began with small talk, and then I shared my news. "Based on what is happening in my life, I can no longer continue my commitment as a Big Sister."

She nodded, looking at me with kindness on her face, and said, "I was afraid you would say that." She was not angry, though; she completely understood. We finished our discussion, and she thanked me for my time, letting me know that I was welcome to reapply in the future. Even though the overall conversation was positive, I still felt guilty for letting down my sponsor, the organization, and my Little

Sister by resigning from my assignment. The program sponsor decided that our weekly activities should end immediately and that notifying all impacted parties should be the next step. In addition to the sponsor's call to my Little Sister's family, I expressed an interest in speaking with the family directly, as I thought it was the responsible thing to do.

I called my Little Sister's home and first spoke with her mother to explain that I would need to withdraw from the program to focus on a family matter that was deeply impacting me. I reassured her that I had a wonderful time getting to know her daughter and stressed that my decision was in no way an expression of negative experiences with her. I asked if I could speak with my Little Sister directly so that I could have a final conversation with her too, and my request was granted. I did not want my Little Sister to internalize my withdrawal as rejection. Without divulging the fact that I was grieving the untimely loss of my brother, I explained that I had to deal with a really serious and unexpected family event and that she would be reassigned to a Big Sister who was better able to fully commit to the assignment. There were several silent pauses on the other end of the line, punctuated by an occasional, "Okay," in acknowledgment of my words. I felt awful about having created a disruption, but I knew that she was not getting the best version of me.

If I'm being honest, I should have resigned from that volunteer role before August, but I was trying my best to fulfill the commitment

I had made before everything happened. I was also in some version of denial, trying to prove to myself that I was, in fact, "okay" and able to function as I did before my brother's death. In hindsight, I also recognize that I was waiting for permission to focus on myself. Back in 1999, very few people were talking about self-care and mental well-being. I felt pressured to rush through grief and resume normal activities and commitments without taking a pause. After all, wasn't it good to carry on with life as if nothing materially changed for me? In my opinion, the answer to that question is no, but back then, I felt required to live as if it were yes.

There is never a convenient time to lose a loved one, and it can happen when you're least expecting it. I lost my brother within two years of my graduating from college, which is, for many, a time marked by promise. My peers were building their lives as carefree, happy, optimistic adults while my reality was crumbling. I, too, had been like them, imagining a life full of happiness and fulfillment. But after my brother's death, I felt uncertain about my path. Things that felt possible now felt out of reach. While others planned weddings, I struggled to sleep without seeing images of my brother's corpse. While others planned career moves, I was planning to attend criminal court proceedings.

After my brother was murdered, I began to doubt the viability of the life I had imagined. Was the propaganda correct? Was I just an inner-city kid destined to repeat the patterns and cycles of others before me? Did I think I could escape the realities of being born in my zip code? Would good things always be beyond my reach? Or would they happen for me, only to be followed by gut-wrenching loss? Trauma planted the smallest seed of doubt, causing me to question the possibility of living a life full of good things. After my brother's murder, everything was different. The world felt smaller; the possibilities felt finite.

As I promised Ma in South Carolina, I visited her in Philadelphia close to three weeks after the funeral, arriving on Thursday with plans to return to North Carolina on Sunday. I wish that I could have stayed longer, but I did not have enough accrued paid time off (PTO) to cover January's extended bereavement leave and this extended weekend visit. I was granted the option to record the number of work hours missed and make up the time when I could. I don't think that a bona fide make-up time policy actually existed, but instead, was created by a compassionate leader who decided to think beyond policy and support a grieving employee during that difficult time. I am so thankful to have been supported by my leaders and peers. I deeply appreciate the flexibility and grace that my employer extended to me.

I spent the seven-hour drive from North Carolina to Philadelphia thinking, reminiscing, and crying. I tried to prepare myself to accept the reality that our family unit had been shattered, shifting us from a family of three to a family of two in the most unsettling way. Ma and I never had one of those mother-daughter relationships propped up as ideal in mainstream movies and media, and for most of my life, our relationship had what I call "dynamics," and those dynamics neither resolve themselves nor magically disappear in times of trauma and loss. Although I wondered how our relationship would change, my mother's well-being was the focus of this visit. This was not intended to be a social trip, and I had only told a couple of people that I would even be in town.

I found a parking spot on the street close to my mom's house and used my key to unlock the front door. I stepped into the living room and greeted Ma with a hug. The house was quiet but not in a comforting, peaceful way. It was the kind of quiet dripping with sadness. A quiet that muffled the joyful sounds of life. In the absence of noise, I was reminded that something was wrong. I pushed through the deafening silence and walked upstairs to put my bag in my room, but as I approached the second-floor landing, I looked toward Keith's bedroom. My room was just a few steps past his and as I made my way down the hall, my stomach felt uneasy. I wanted to peek inside his room and occupy his space, but his door was closed. So, I put my bag in my room first and then went back to his door, twisting the handle only to be met with resistance. Ma had locked it. Maybe it was easier that way—otherwise, she might feel the urge to open the door and sit in the sadness of his empty room as I was. I inhaled and exhaled as if to reset myself, then walked back downstairs.

I tried to make myself useful, wanting to dive into whatever looked like a task waiting to be finished, and thought dishes were a good place to start. But there were no dirty dishes to wash. Aside from the buttered toast that likely accompanied Ma's morning cup of coffee, I detected no signs of cooking. I scanned the rest of the room in an attempt to find any busy work needing to be done and found a stack of sympathy cards from well-wishers sitting on the dining table for me to read. I read them all and was moved by the number of cards that were from former teachers, staff, and administrators from Keith's and my school. Knowing that I was looking for something to do and seeing me now read the cards she had set aside for me, Ma asked me to complete and address the stack of "Thank You" cards. Ma's penmanship was so much better than mine, but I did my best.

We chatted while I completed my task, and I asked her if I could help sort through Keith's things. She quickly shook her head and replied, "No, no." She stood and walked over to the secretary. "I saved his hat if you want it. His coat was ruined by the bullet holes. He was wearing this..." Ma said as she handed me a plain black beanie, telling me that the blood stains came out after washing it a couple of times. I thanked her and held the hat tightly. Certainly, there were other personal belongings in his room that she would want me to have, right? My mind fixated on the "No, no" that she quickly issued at my request to help organize his room, but I realized that this was not the time to press the matter.

During my first evening there, a friend who had helped me through personal difficulties a few years prior visited my mom and me after work. It was good to see someone to whom I neither needed to qualify my suffering nor contextualize myself. I did not need to steel myself in anticipation of questions regarding Keith's occupation or extra-curricular activities; she was not going to engage in the victim-blaming that had already become all too common in just those first few weeks. It felt good to remove the mask and be myself. As we talked in the living room, Ma had fallen asleep on the couch. I guess something was comforting about the physical presence and sounds of others in the house again. My friend noticed and decided that she should be getting home. I walked her outside to her car and then stood on the porch as she drove away.

As I was waving goodbye, I could see a tall man walking on the sidewalk in my direction. As he got closer to the house, I recognized his face—he was one of my brother's friends from the neighborhood, living only a couple of houses down the street. I had not seen him in close to five years, but he looked the same, just with a full beard now.

I originally thought he intended to visit Ma to offer his condolences, but after some pleasantries, I could tell he hadn't heard the news yet. Sure enough, after a few minutes together, he asked me the question that I knew was coming but was not ready to answer. "Um, I haven't seen Keith in a while. Is he okay?" The weather was frightfully cold that night, so I invited him inside to talk. I needed to buy time to think of what to say. I led him inside, and since Ma was still sleeping on the couch, we sat at the dining table. I didn't offer him anything to eat or drink, instead, the next words I told him were, "Someone shot Keith."

"What hospital is he in?" he asked me, clearly shocked.

I kept it together and explained in a surprising calm, "Keith didn't make it. We buried him in South Carolina." I watched as his friend tried to absorb the news. He rested one elbow on the table and put his hand on his forehead, rubbing it while choking back tears. I didn't know what to say. I didn't expect to be consoling someone else so soon after my brother's murder. After a while, he composed himself, offered his sympathies, and asked me to pass a message to my mom when she woke up. I agreed, and then he left the house. I watched him walk down the block until he arrived at his home.

I went back inside and sat on the couch while Ma continued to sleep. The television was on, but I wasn't paying it much attention. Sitting on the couch started to feel like old times. I kept turning my head to the left and looking at the front door, waiting to hear my brother's key turn the lock. Waiting to see him walk through the front door. Waiting to hear his footsteps on the hardwood floor. I must have done that for an hour. He's really not coming back, I thought.

I woke Ma and offered to help her upstairs to bed, but afterward, because I still found nighttime to be insufferable, I returned to the living room to sit a little longer. Falling and remaining asleep had been difficult those last few weeks, so I always prolonged it as much as possible. In the silence, I looked around the room at the family pictures wondering how we were supposed to function after this. Keith was my mother's firstborn. He was my first friend. At those thoughts, I wept quietly so as not to wake Ma. I stayed in the living room for another hour then gathered myself and went upstairs to prepare for bed. I woke up the next morning feeling more refreshed than I had in weeks; I actually slept well. Sometimes, a good cry leads to a good night's sleep.

For the rest of the trip, Ma and I avoided the obvious. On Saturday, Ma even encouraged me to get out for a while and meet up with friends. I politely declined the offer. Saturday marked the three-week anniversary of Keith's death, so spending time celebrating anything was the furthest thing from my mind. But even though I stayed home for the day, we still didn't talk about my brother. We also discussed very little about the criminal justice implications and information from the District Attorney's office. Honestly, I had no idea what to say for fear that it would cause Ma to cry. It's never easy seeing your mom cry, especially when there's nothing you can do to stop the underlying pain. So I could only hope that my physical presence could offer some semblance of short-term comfort.

In the silence that often found its way between Ma and me, my mind kept wandering to my brother's room. I wanted so badly to be in his space, to feel close to him before I returned home. What was behind the locked door? And why did Ma quickly decline my help to sort through his things? So, during one of the days that Ma fell asleep downstairs again, I decided to search for the key. I was not willing to creep down the creaky stairs and risk awakening Ma, so I limited my search to the second floor, specifically the two bedrooms with unlocked doors. Because it was easier, I started my search in the dressers in my room, but to no avail. I then tiptoed to the other side of the hall to Ma's bedroom. On her dresser was a small glass bowl full of trinkets, paper clips, and a few bronze coins. It was there that I saw the key. I exhaled with relief then walked apprehensively to Keith's room. After a moment, I unlocked the door. Before I even entered, I saw that Ma had stripped the linen from his bed, exposing a pristine white mattress. I slowly walked inside. Although the furniture remained untouched, dark trash bags full of his clothing sat on the floor, and the personal effects that rested on the tops of the nightstand and dresser were gone. I sat at the foot of the bed and looked out the window into the barren backyard. I wept. I could not believe that my brother was gone.

In Philadelphia, misdemeanors and felonies move through many steps of the criminal justice process.[1] The first two steps—reporting of a crime and making an arrest—occurred the day my brother was murdered on a side street near a busy intersection. The third step involves the District Attorney's Charging Unit drafting the criminal complaint, which lists charges and summarizes the factual basis for the charges. The fourth step, a preliminary arraignment, happens within hours of arrest. A bail commissioner presides over a preliminary arraignment to advise the defendant of the charges in the criminal complaint, inform the defendant of his/her right to a lawyer, and schedule a preliminary hearing date for felonies or a trial date for misdemeanors.[2] A preliminary hearing is like a trial but at a much earlier stage in the criminal justice process. Preliminary hearings serve an important purpose: they force prosecutors to present a prima facie case, or probable cause that the person being charged has committed the crime they are being charged with.[3] If the court does not see that there is enough evidence to come close to obtaining a conviction, it will dismiss the case and spare the defendant the time, energy, and stress that comes with a prolonged trial.[4]

The last four steps of the process, trials and hearings, deliberations, case outcomes, and appeals (if applicable), occurred during the

---

1   "Criminal Justice Process - Office of the District Attorney: City of Philadelphia."

2   IBID.

3   "Philadelphia Preliminary Hearing Lawyer | Preliminary Hearing Attorney in Pennsylvania."

4   IBID.

second half of 1999. In early spring, a Philadelphia police officer con-tacted me about the trials regarding my brother's murder, saying he was interested in scheduling trial dates for the co-defendants. I was shocked at the timing of the call, as I assumed it would take a year or so before the trial process started. I had wanted more time so that I could go into the court proceedings feeling prepared and in control of my emotions, but in the spring, my brain was still squishy, and the reality of my brother's loss was still slowly sinking in.

Nonetheless, the trial dates were set for early summer, with each co-defendant to be tried separately. The officer mailed me three sub-poenas to share with my employer to substantiate my need for time away: one for each co-defendant's trial dates and another for the an-ticipated sentencing hearing in the fall. A couple of short months lat-er, I was on my way back to Philadelphia for the beginning of the trial for the first co-defendant, set for June 28. I had no idea what to ex-pect. The morning of, Ma and I quietly rode the subway downtown to the courthouse. It seems that we continued our unspoken agreement to not talk about Keith.

When we arrived at the courthouse, Ma and I met a wonderful ad-vocate assigned to us by a local victim advocacy and services program. She met us at the courthouse, sat with us every day, and answered all of our random questions about the court proceedings that were expected to last a week. The Assistant District Attorney (ADA) intro-duced himself that first day as well and provided an overview of the proceedings. I tried my best to listen and absorb all of the important pieces of information, but my mind and emotions were so scrambled. What I could catch was the reminder from the ADA that the co-defendants would be tried separately, and the activities of each successive day were predicated on the outcomes of the prior day. Court proceedings began around 10 a.m., but there was a lot of idle time during the day, which added to my anguish and anxiety.

The courtroom was open, airy, and sparsely populated, but the appreciated space that I felt quickly evaporated. As Ma and I sat behind the prosecutor's table, the door to the left of the judge's bench opened, revealing a man wearing handcuffs. I felt an intense shock of heat on the back of my neck that quickly grew and spread to my face. I had never felt anger like that. I felt sick to my stomach. The handcuffed man walked to the table where the defense attorneys sat. I was surprised to see there was no partition separating the prosecutor's table from the defense attorney's table. I immediately thought *I could jump over the banister and run to the table...* and *the bailiff is out of shape—I could get there before him.* But then I looked at Ma. Had I acted on that instinct to approach the table, the ensuing chaos would have only added to her stress. Moreover, both co-defendants had already shown they lacked impulse control and sound decision-making. Ma and I were living the painful consequences of such actions, so exercising restraint was critical at that moment.

I forced myself to calm down and focus on the trial. To help shift my mindset, I removed the small notebook from my purse, eager to take notes, but my desire to record the details of the day's proceedings inspired the ire of the bailiff, who angrily walked toward me, shouting that I could not take notes. I was already feeling fragile and anxious, and now, I felt small. Where was the compassion? Being in court daily was his job. For me, this was a new experience and certainly not one for which I was prepared. I put the book away and remembered to get the stenographer's business card at the end of the day to request a transcript of what she typed.

Three days' worth of expert and witness testimony was emotionally exhausting. On the third day, the judge rendered a guilty verdict of third-degree murder for the first co-defendant. Based on the defendant's signed confession and the evidence presented, Ma and I were disappointed that the judge did not convict him of first-degree murder. In Pennsylvania, first and second-degree murder convictions lead to hefty sentences, like life imprisonment with no possibility of parole or the death penalty. We felt that the ADA made a decision that significantly affected the outcome: agreeing to each co-defendant's request to waive a jury trial in exchange for a judge trial. In a judge trial, which is also called a bench trial, there is no jury, and the judge decides the facts of the case and applies the law. We believed that members of a jury would have been more sympathetic to our case than a judge and would have rendered a stronger verdict that carried a stronger penalty. Instead, defense attorneys for the co-defendants were extended the opportunity to present their respective cases to the assigned presiding judge.

Back on the first day of court proceedings for the first co-defendant, Ma and I asked the ADA about when the trial for the second co-defendant would begin. After a significant delay, the Assistant District Attorney reemerged with disappointing news: the second co-defendant accepted a plea agreement of third-degree murder. In a plea deal, the prosecution and defense attorneys arrive at the terms of the agreement. The terms frequently involve the prosecuting attorney (in our case, the Assistant District Attorney) in exchange for the defendant's plea of guilty or nolo contendere, promising concessions such as a reduction of a charge to a lesser offense, the dropping of one or more additional charges, a recommendation of a lenient sentence, or a combination of these.[5] All terms of the agreement are openly acknowledged for the judge's assessment.[6] Other than the third-degree charge, we were given no other details about the deal. The second co-defendant was a repeat felony offender who had been arrested almost four years prior for the commission of multiple crimes and then was placed in a juvenile detention center. The repeat felony offender was released from juvenile detention just ten months before ambushing my brother. Based on witness testimony, Ma and I felt that he, too, should have received a stronger conviction than third-degree murder.

5   "234 Pa. Code Rule 590. Pleas and Plea Agreements."

6   IBID.

There would be no trial for the second co-defendant; his sentencing hearing would be our first and only time meeting the judge presiding over the case.

The ADA told us that we could spend the next two months preparing victim impact statements to present to the judges, as long as we turned them in by September 23. He explained that victim impact statements describe the emotional, physical, and financial impact homicide survivors have suffered as a direct result of the crime. Bereaved family members may also leverage the impact statement to ask the Court to sentence an offender to the maximum allowable prison term. Almost three months after the first hearing, in September, we received the most important piece of information: prison terms for both co-defendants. Ma and I had submitted our statements ahead of the sentencing date and received a promise that we would also be allowed to read our statements to both judges.

I returned to Philadelphia in September for sentencing and on the morning of, Ma and I met with the judge presiding over the case of the second co-defendant, the repeat felony offender who had accepted a plea agreement. I was surprised by Ma's composure and poise as she delivered her impact statement first. I was the complete opposite, crying and stumbling over my words. Thankfully, the judge was patient as I struggled to read my statement in its entirety. After further deliberation, the judge issued the prison sentence, taking into account the second co-defendant's prior record score and the recommendations offered by the Assistant District Attorney: twenty-two and a half to forty-five years with parole eligibility after serving the sentence minimum.

After our lunch break, we met with the judge—a different judge—presiding over the first co-defendant's case. Just like before, we read our impact statements. Then, the judge issued his closing remarks before delivering the prison term. Something he said struck a sour note with me; he expressed gratitude for the safety of his children and confessed an uncertainty in his ability to move through this kind of adversity. I don't begrudge anyone's ability to live in a safe community, and I celebrate the safety of one's children, but I do feel that these statements were ill-timed, insulting, and inappropriate. Sentencing is not the time to laud homicide survivors for their strength. The judge continued and issued the prison sentence for the first co-defendant: twenty to forty years with parole eligibility after serving the sentence minimum.

After the court adjourned, the ADA answered our questions, the most important of which related to the likelihood of early release. The Assistant District Attorney reassured Ma and me that neither co-defendant would be paroled before serving his respective sentence minimum. *Good*, I thought, but Ma looked at the ADA and said, "I won't be here in twenty years." Then, she turned to me and said, "Kim, you'll have to do it." I knew by "it," Ma was referring to meeting with the Parole Board in twenty and twenty-two-and-a-half years, respectively. Ma was a healthy fifty-one-year-old, so I was taken aback by her assertion, but I merely nodded, unable to project that far into the future. I was focused only on that moment, breathing a sigh of relief that both co-defendants would be serving substantial time. The Assistant District Attorney encouraged us both to register with Pennsylvania's notification program to ensure that we were alerted of the inmates' movements and parole eligibility. I enrolled as soon as I received the instructions.

The holiday season was quickly approaching, and I was dreading it. I was still counting the loss of my brother in weeks. This year was full of painful "firsts" without Keith, and as difficult as it was to broach the topic of holiday planning, I wanted to start the conversation with Ma so that I could begin to adjust my own schedule and request time off. During the holiday season, people often look forward to going home to enjoy family traditions, food, and fellowship but I expected none of that this year. Much like February, I was only concerned about Ma's feelings of loneliness and sadness during the first Thanksgiving.

During one of our early October conversations, I finally inquired about Thanksgiving and whether she had any initial thoughts about where and how she wanted to spend it. Ma's reply left me a bit deflated. "Thanksgiving is just another day, and I have nothing to be thankful for." My head understood the reason for the reply, so I compartmentalized my feelings. Admittedly, given the magnitude of the loss, it was difficult to have a posture of gratitude. But my heart still needed a mother's tenderness. Her statement also agitated my long-held belief that my brother was her favorite. And as I said before, relationship dynamics neither improve nor disappear in the face of grief.

I drove up to Philadelphia the day before Thanksgiving and as I entered her house, remembering her comment only months before, I was surprised to see that she made efforts to create a sense of warmth. I didn't ask what changed her mind or tell her how that comment made me feel. Ma and I never expressed difficult emotions to each other; we avoided having transparent conversations about our feelings. Nonetheless, we had the best Thanksgiving that we could have, and I was content with that.

I never imagined living in a world without my brother. After he died, I lost my joy. I approached each day as if it were something to be suffered, not celebrated. For a short while, I decided that I would try and make the most of each day, even if I had to "will" it. I would get out of bed immediately after the alarm sounded, determined to have a great day and greet each morning with positivity. Today, that behavior would be described as toxic positivity, a dysfunctional emotional management response that demands happiness even in negative or difficult situations. In either case, my attempt at toxic positivity was short-lived; grief and depression were too powerful to be suppressed. Admittedly, it was naive to think that I should "will" myself to feel better. I had experienced deep loss and deserved the time and space to acknowledge, process, and express my emotions. But it was only in the second year after losing my brother that I realized that and began thinking about my physical safety and my family unit, my place within it, and my future as my mom's only remaining child.

A Cold Winter

1. Generally speaking, what coping mechanisms do you lean on during stressful situations?

   ☐ Physical (dance, exercise, walk, etc.).
   ☐ Spiritual/Healing Modalities (organized religion, spiritual texts, meditation).
   ☐ Creative/Expressive Arts.
   ☐ Other.

2. How has using those coping mechanisms helped?

3. How are you expressing your anger?

   ☐ What resources are you using to support your grieving process (ie, therapy from trauma-informed specialists, counseling, books, support groups, friends, etc.)?

   ☐ How have they helped?

4. Have you been assigned a counselor or victim service advocate by a state or local agency? Are you in contact with the counselor or advocate? How has that helped?

5. If necessary, do you have age-appropriate resources for children impacted by the loss?

6. What kind of conversations are you having with other bereaved family members?

7. Do you need resources to help you navigate conversations?

8. Does your employer offer any resources that you can leverage, like mental health days, paid time off, short-term leave, employee assistance programs, etc.?

9. Have you researched whether any resources provided by your local municipality, county, or state exist? If applicable, have you leveraged those resources?

10. Are you feeling pressure to remain involved in all of the activities that were on your plate before your loved one's death?

11. Have you considered temporarily taking time away from essential and/or non-essential activities to invest in your wellness?

12. Should you decide to take time away, who can help you create a communication/exit plan?

13. How has the loss impacted your relationship with your current partner or spouse?

14. Do you feel supported by your spouse or partner?

15. If you are single, have you continued dating or meeting new prospective romantic partners?

16. How do you believe your family's dynamics are impacting:

    ☐   How you express your feelings?
    ☐   With whom you express your overall feelings?
    ☐   Your overall healing journey?

17. How do you think this trauma has impacted how you view yourself?

18. Is your self-talk affirming or negative?

19. How have you been sleeping? If not well, have you adopted routines that aid you?

20. How are you doing today?

REFLECTIONS:

PART II

A Hopeful Spring

CHAPTER FOUR

"Are You Okay?"

The years ticked by, and I counted the holidays and birthdays that passed. I counted each year hoping that "this one" would coincide with an end to the pain. I was waiting for the heaviness to lift so that I could resume living my life. I mean, after three years, I should feel better, right? But every year, when the anniversary of my brother's death approached, my body would tense, as if bracing for the impact of the pain that would accompany it. *Should it take this long to feel like myself again?*

It was a beautiful spring day in 2018. The sun was shining, and the sky was a picture-perfect shade of blue. I slowly walked to the mailbox so that I could enjoy the breeze, as I knew that this lovely spring day would soon be replaced by the stifling triple-digit heat for which Texas is known. As I returned to the front door, I scanned and shuffled the envelopes in my hands. Mostly junk mail, as usual. At the bottom of the pile, however, was a thick envelope with a familiar image of a keystone in the top left with the words "Pennsylvania Office of the Victim Advocate" next to it. I stood there on the driveway looking at the envelope. My feet felt like stone; a knot formed in my stomach. The lightness of the day had given way to heaviness. Was it time already? Deep down, I knew that the date was approaching, but I wasn't ready to receive this letter. Not today.

Around 1999, roughly sixty percent of homicides that occurred in Philadelphia were unsolved, according to the police officer I spoke with when scheduling the trial dates. Thanks to a passenger on the nearby elevated (el) train and rapid responses by Philadelphia police dispatchers and officers, the people responsible for murdering my brother were apprehended. Because of the modest number of homicide cases in which perpetrators were identified, the co-defendants moved through the criminal justice system rather quickly. Despite evidence that pointed to the fact that this crime was pre-meditated and should have been a first-degree felony charge, both co-defendants were convicted of third-degree murder, implying that they didn't intentionally mean to cause harm to my brother.

So, when I received that envelope from the Office of the Victim Advocate in 2018, I knew that it signaled parole eligibility for the first co-defendant—the inmate with the shorter minimum sentence. How could two decades have passed so quickly? My brother's death felt like an event that simultaneously happened a lifetime ago, yet one that occurred just yesterday. I had seemingly moved forward in time, advancing the calendar, but in that instant, as I held that envelope, I was transported back to 1999, and my old pals, grief and depression, found me again. I felt like I was occupying both past and present, and the worst part was that I was alone. Both Ma and Mr. Joe had predeceased me. I felt like a tiny ant trying to carry incredible weight. Ma's voice echoed, "I won't be here... Kim, you'll have to do it," and I remembered thinking that was a ridiculous statement, that, of course, she would still be here.

Parole is the release of an inmate from prison before his or her sentence's maximum date but can only be granted after the minimum sentence date.[7] In Pennsylvania, preparation starts approximately eight months before an inmate's minimum sentence date.[8] During that time, multiple data points are collected from a variety of sources, including a pre-parole interview and assessment of the inmate, a case review of the inmate's behavior while incarcerated, an inmate's risk score, the survivor's input (also called a testimony or presentation), and an interview with the inmate.[9] The purpose of the survivor's testimony is to provide information about the continuing nature and extent of any physical harm, psychological harm, or emotional trauma as a result of the crime. Survivors' input is optional, but the other data points are required.[10] Pennsylvania's Parole Board consists of nine members, including a Chairman, appointed by the Governor with the advice and consent of the Senate.[11] The Parole Board makes parole and parole revocation decisions by a majority of the Parole Board or

7   "Parole 101."
8   IBID.
9   IBID.
10 "Parole Interview."
11 "Decision Makers - Parole Process."

in panels of two persons. Panels consist of one Parole Board member and one Hearing Examiner or two Parole Board members.[12] The parole process is best described as a series of sequential steps for both the inmate as he or she prepares for the parole interview and the Parole Board as it reviews and processes hundreds of cases each month.[13]

I held the envelope for a while before opening it, but when I did, I saw that the envelope contained a letter, a pamphlet about Pennsylvania's Office of the Victim Advocate (OVA), and directions to their office in Harrisburg. My heart and mind struggled to process the words that my eyes were scanning so I read the letter twice. At the bottom of the first page, the name and phone number of a member of the OVA team were listed with instructions to call and schedule the date and time that I wanted to give my testimony to the Parole Board panel. I was not ready to call OVA. Feeling overwhelmed, I needed to get out of the house for some air. I needed to run a few errands anyway, so I folded the letter and placed it in my purse, wanting to keep it close in case I mustered the courage to call while sitting in my car between stops.

During my stop at a nearby gas station, I found the courage to call the OVA. My heart was pounding and my hands were shaking, but when I dialed the number, I got the voicemail. I was relieved that I would not be speaking to someone, so I listened carefully as the voicemail said to state my name and phone number, the inmate's name

12   IBID.
13   "The Pennsylvania Parole Process."

or number, and the reason for my call. I took a deep breath and began speaking slowly. I was able to verbalize my name and number, but while saying the name of the inmate, I began to cry. I quickly pressed the "End" button on my cell phone. *At least I was able to leave my name and number*, I thought. Hopefully, my message was intelligible, and someone would return my call.

Later in the day, after all my errands were finished and I was back at home, a woman who identified herself as my advocate returned my call. Her voice was soothing as she introduced herself, and I immediately felt more at ease with her. I told her my name again and the reason why I had called. I was proud that I held it together to communicate the purpose of my call this time. I even apologized for having had an emotional breakdown while leaving a voicemail.

And then, quite curtly, she asked, "Are you okay?" The coldness in her tone felt familiar, but the abrupt switch in her demeanor was confusing. I answered in the affirmative, being careful not to show further emotion to her. Recognizing that I lived in another state, my advocate asked if I wanted to visit Harrisburg to deliver my testimony in person or via telephone. Given the impact of the outcome, it was important to me to physically be there to persuade the Parole Board to deny the inmate's parole request. Without hesitation, I confirmed my plan to travel to Harrisburg and deliver my testimony in person.

After the call, I realized that I was not okay. I was caught off guard after reading the OVA's letter but still felt obligated to say that yes, I was okay, for the sake of the phone call. Our exchange bothered me for the next few days; I tried to shake her question off, but unsuccessfully. Nineteen years ago, when people made rude comments, asked judgmental questions, or wanted to engage in victim-blaming, I shut down. I needed to finally speak up. So, I called the OVA and requested another advocate. After hearing about my experience, I received an apology and was quickly assigned a different advocate. I felt relieved and could more easily focus.

By the end of my testimony to the Parole Board panel, I was able to articulate why I found the question "Are you okay?" bothersome—aside from the harsh tone with which it was asked. I expected an advocate for homicide survivors to have a basic understanding of how this loss affects surviving loved ones. The delivery of the question and, given the circumstances under which we were speaking, asking the question "Are you okay?" suggested a lack of compassion, interpersonal skills, and knowledge about the realities of the continuing effects of trauma. Continuing a relationship with this advocate felt unsafe and too risky for my fragile state. I shared that feedback during my testimony and am pleased that the OVA seemed appreciative of this and other feedback that I expressed.

CHAPTER FIVE

Loss by Traumatic Means

I had twelve weeks to prepare and deliver my testimony to the Parole Board panel. I thought back to the victim impact statement that I tried to deliver nineteen years earlier and how I had become too overcome with emotion to articulate my statement in the way I wanted. Now, I was determined to give a cogent testimony to the panel. My first step was to brainstorm, to think about what I wanted to convey to the parole board members. My mind was all over the place, and to my surprise, so were my emotions. I was already struggling. I felt like I was drowning in grief—a grief that was layered and resolute in its intensity. A grief that was isolating and, at times, overpowering. I didn't expect to feel this way after nearly two decades. Was something wrong with me?

My mind returned to the two-year mark when the pain of loss felt sharper than the first. I think it's because I had moved out of that protective, out-of-body cocoon and returned to the real world. On the second anniversary, I called in sick and stayed home to allow myself the space to tend to any heavy feelings that surfaced. I was later told that a co-worker's response to my need for self-care on the second anniversary of my brother's death was less than compassionate. "It's been two years. Kim isn't over that *yet?*" It reminded me of one of the ministers at a Dallas church who told me that after seven years, I should be "over that" by now. *So, why at the nineteen-year mark am I feeling this pain so intensely?*

Turning my attention to something I knew I could handle, I decided to secure my travel plans. Three days before my testimony, I planned to fly into Philadelphia, rent a car, stay in a hotel to fine-tune my speech, and then drive to Harrisburg the morning of the fourteenth for the Parole Board panel. I viewed this as a stealth mission; my goal was to arrive safely, deliver the strongest address to the panel, and then return to Dallas. I did not intend to visit a bunch of family and friends while in the area.

A dear friend in Philadelphia had been emotionally supportive throughout my preparation and instrumental in helping me secure hotel accommodations. Although she wanted to, work constraints prevented her from riding with me to Harrisburg on the day of the testimony. She felt terrible that I would be driving to and from Harrisburg alone and encouraged me to consider inviting a relative in the area to accompany me. I knew that the day would be difficult, heavy, and evoke a variety of feelings, so I appreciated her advice. The best person to join me would be someone who had already demonstrated a mix of competencies befitting the circumstance, so after a few days of contemplation, the name of a relative came to mind.

During other personal inflection points in my life, this relative had expressed the desire to be supportive, so I had no doubts that she would be more than willing to join me for this step. I called and told her about my upcoming Parole Board testimony, asking if she could come with me to Harrisburg. With misplaced enthusiasm, she expressed interest in going, telling me that she had always wanted to study Criminal Justice. I hoped for a reaction that reflected her ability to view the trip from my perspective—one that acknowledged the gravity of the situation and a curiosity about what I might need (a sincere "How can I help you?" would have been nice). Instead, I felt that there was interest in going along for the ride to Harrisburg solely to watch a presentation to the Parole Board in real-time.

I thought back to the trial days when a man walked into the courtroom because he wanted to observe and listen to a criminal case. He sat there for close to ten minutes before he was noticed and escorted out. Over the years, it has been my experience that many people want to feast on the circumstances surrounding the death of my brother, consuming the details of the crime and disregarding my pain like picked-over bones. Some listeners were even looking to place blame. Others were looking for details to confirm the assumptions they may have already made about my brother only knowing contextual information: he was a young black male living in an urban setting. The victim-blaming and victim-shaming were heartbreaking, tiring, and infuriating.

Needless to say, I was deeply disappointed by her reaction. Providing testimony to a Parole Board panel is neither the time to play out one's career aspirations nor to observe the presentation as if it were an episode of a television show. In my experience, emotionally stressful events require either supportive, compassionate people or no one at all. I chose to go alone and told her that I would prefer to call her after the Parole Board panel.

As I continued to try to write my presentation, and as silly as it sounds, I decided to Google *how long does the grieving process take after the death of a loved one?* I read countless articles and book excerpts echoing the notion that healing from grief follows a specific timeline. But neither my feelings nor experiences aligned with the classic stages of grief paradigms that I read. Those articles focused more on bereavement following the death of a loved one due to natural causes.

I altered my search. When I found articles and abstracts that referenced terms and phrases like "grief that feels different from other losses" and "complex trauma," I felt as if my feelings nineteen years post-loss were immediately validated. I was astounded by the information that I found. According to the articles, I was considered a co-victim, co-survivor, or homicide survivor. Per the Office for Victims of Crime, these terms describe anyone impacted by a loved one's death due to homicide.[14] These survivors feel the life-changing impact of the trauma, hardship, and loss that results from the crime.[15]

14 "Homicide Victims/Co-Survivors | Office for Victims of Crime." 2020.
15 IBID.

Homicide is considered a loss by traumatic means and a traumatic stressor, and homicide survivors have a higher risk of post-traumatic stress disorder (PTSD).[16,17] Authors of other articles cited that homicide survivors are at risk for complicated grief, depression, and anxiety.[18] Moreover, homicide survivors face the stigma associated with homicide bereavement.[19] Researchers found a high degree of overlap across multiple categories, with nearly all of the PTSD—positive cases screening positive for complicated grief and depression. Levels of complicated grief and depression did not differ significantly between those early and late in bereavement.[20] I was most excited to read that time since homicide was not significantly associated with either depression or complicated grief.[21] Based on the research that I had read, there was no evidence to substantiate the notion that I should have gotten over the grief by now.

16 Green BL. Traumatic loss: Conceptual and empirical links between trauma and bereavement. Journal of Personal and Interpersonal Loss. 2000; 5:1–17.

17 Green BL, Krupnick JL, Stockton P, Goodman L, Corcoran C, Petty R. Psychological outcomes associated with traumatic loss in a sample of young women. American Behavioral Scientist. 2001;44: 817–837.

18 Rynearson Edward K., McCreery JM. Bereavement after homicide: a synergism of trauma and loss. Am J Psychiatry. 1993 Feb;150(2):258-61. Doi: 10.1176/ajp.150.2.258. PMID: 8422076.

19 McDevitt-Murphy, Meghan E., Neimeyer, Robert A., Burke, Laurie A., Williams, Joah A., & Lawson, Katherine (2012). The Toll of Traumatic Loss in African Americans Bereaved by Homicide. Psychological Trauma: Theory, Research, Practice, and Policy, 4(3), 303–311.

20 Zinzow, Heidi, Rheingold Alyssa A., Hawkins Alesia, Saunders Benjamin, Kilpatrick Dean G. Losing a loved one to homicide: prevalence and mental health correlates in a national sample of young adults. J Trauma Stress. 2009 Feb; 22(1): 20-7.

21 IBID.

As odd as it may sound, learning all of this made me perk up. It was so validating to read these conceptualizations of homicide. Instead of believing that something was wrong with me for still having profound sadness, the authors of these articles provided language and alternative lenses through which I could understand and verbalize my grief and lived experiences. I wish I had been exposed to this information earlier in my grief journey. Professionals whose work puts them near homicide survivors seemed unaware of these concepts. I wish that onboarding programs for employees of the District Attorney's Office and the Pennsylvania Office of the Victim Advocate included this information. What they may not have realized is that this lack of knowledge and adequate training puts survivors' well-being at risk. People and places that should have felt safe, restorative, and empathetic left much to be desired.

I had always assumed that the average human being possessed a modicum of compassion, but my experiences during the years closely following my brother's death, however, have disavowed me of that notion. I was taken aback by how often Ma and I routinely experienced rudeness and comments that insinuated Keith was at fault for what happened and that we were less entitled to grieve because of that. Close to three years after my brother's murder, I was telling Ma about a fantastic support group that I found in North Carolina where I had met courageous people who openly shared their experiences and encouraged each other. For as long as I could remember, Ma had never been fond of communicating her feelings with family members, so I knew the chances of her wanting to talk to strangers about her feelings associated with the loss of her son were slim. I knew that she would benefit from receiving the compassion and support that she had needed for so long, so I hoped that by sharing my positive experience with the group, she would be inspired to try.

In response, she instead told me about the District Attorney's Office's invitation to join a support group. "Do you know where this support group meets?" she asked. I was prepared for her to tell me a location far across town or somewhere else with impossible logistics. The location was much worse than that. "The morgue. They meet at the morgue," she said before I could even put together a real guess. I could not believe it. Many parents, like Ma, went to the morgue to identify the corpses of their dead children, so the mere thought of going back to that place—a literal reminder of the death of their loved one—to then talk about the death of their loved one, no doubt caused post-traumatic stress.

During a different conversation, Ma told me about an interaction that she had with another grieving mother who had buried two sons within two years. Both of her sons were murdered, and the family buried them in the same cemetery. One day, this grieving mother received a call from a cemetery staff member, who commented on her recent "purchases." The staff member asked the grieving mother if she might be interested in purchasing a third plot at a discounted rate. Motivated by greed, this cemetery staffer disregarded the feelings of a bereaved woman to advance his financial objectives. Maybe I'm wrong, but I don't think a mother living in an affluent zip code would have received a call from someone offering a deal on a burial plot. "Nobody cares," Ma said. Based on her experiences and the experiences of other homicide survivors, that was a logical conclusion.

Amid this swell of emotions and Google searches, I continued preparing my testimony. I wanted to paint a full picture of the continuing effect of my brother's homicide on our lives and ask the panel to deny this request for parole, so I wrote my thoughts on paper and then organized them in an outline. It was important to humanize my brother to the Board members so they didn't see him as just another number, so I gathered as many pictures as I could to incorporate into the PowerPoint presentation and included stories and personal details about him. I also felt compelled to share what I knew of Ma's experience regarding how the loss impacted her too. I was so thankful to have the court transcripts from all those years ago. I had been carrying these four books around for years—from apartment to apartment, from state to state. The transcripts always traveled close to me in the car, never in a U-Haul.

Once, in my early years of grief, I opened the first volume, but roughly three pages in, I began to cry. I closed it and hoped that one day, I would have the fortitude to read its contents. No matter where I have lived, these four books always rested on the bottom corner of my bookcase. Close enough for me to reach them if necessary, but far enough not to entice me. I would glance at them occasionally as if I were checking my readiness to reread and would retreat when I got the feeling that it was still not time. But preparing my testimony for the Parole Board panel was an opportune time for me to retry. I wanted to deliver a rich, factually dense presentation to the panel, and I wanted to represent Ma's perspective as best as I could. Ready to dissect the text with pen and highlighter in hand, I picked up the first volume. I covered a lot of ground compared to the three pages I was only able to read before, but reading witness accounts, a ballistics expert's testimony, and my brother's last words had become too much. I learned that I could only consume the details in small bites before needing to step away and breathe. Thankfully, I had twelve weeks to prepare.

As the days progressed, familiar signs of stress and anxiety were present. I made unhealthy food choices by foregoing healthier snack options in favor of processed foods. More frequently, I paired sparkling white wine with anything that I ate. My insomnia returned. When I did manage to sleep, I had intense nightmares. I struggled to quiet my mind, and I was desperate for relief. Nonetheless, my testimony began to take form. I edited my draft several times. And even though controlling and arranging the words on paper proved much easier than quelling the chaos in my mind and body, I knew, just like that second year, I also needed to prioritize self-care.

My internet searches on survivor grief led me to articles that outlined the emotional and physical benefits of meditation, so I decided to give it a try. In my most comfortable and supportive chair, I sat in the lotus position with my arms relaxed and breathed deeply for as long as I could. To help clear the clutter from my mind, I visualized myself sitting as I was in that moment and watching beams of white light swirling around and through me. I breathed deeply and imagined peace and calm hugging my body like a shawl. I decided to begin each day leading up to the Parole Board panel with meditation to focus my breath and set intentions to accomplish one or two goals that day. I was so pleased when I began to experience the benefits.

After a week of daily meditation, I felt ready to manage the physical manifestations of my emotional and mental anguish. Growing up, I was called a "tomboy," a label used to describe girls whose behavior was considered more masculine—or boyish—than feminine. In my case, that behavior included a preference for engaging in active, physical play. Albeit comical to Ma, in my opinion, returning home smelling like a puppy was a sign of time well spent outside. Just as it was when I was a kid, physical movement has been critical for my well-being into adulthood. I always felt better after exercising, especially when physical or mental sluggishness preceded the exercise. I instinctively knew when my body needed to move too. In addition to the physical benefits, movement has been shown to improve mental health by reducing anxiety, improving cognitive function, and alleviating depressive symptoms and negative mood.[22] Despite my strong desire to remain home and work through my emotions in private, I knew that I needed to leave my protective cocoon and get some exercise. So, I decided to return to regular workouts at the gym close to my home.

I remember how lethargic I felt as I walked into the gym. A year or so prior, I had purchased personal training sessions with a trainer who worked at a gym location across town and wanted to inquire about their transferability. I had only used half of the sessions, and I did not want to forfeit what was remaining. The grief must have shown on my face because the manager furrowed his brows and invited me to sit in the office. Before addressing my questions about the personal training sessions, he expressed interest in my well-being, showed concern, and offered prayer and words of comfort. I was an emotional wreck, which was visible to this club manager whom I had met only a few moments earlier. This stranger's expressions of curiosity and compassion amazed me. The manager informed me that the balance of the personal training sessions that I purchased was transferrable and that I could begin working with a trainer in that location. He then invited a trainer into the office and made the introductions before the trainer and I moved to a private area to complete an intake session. We discussed my motivation for working out, fitness goals, and availability to exercise.

22 "Depression and anxiety: Exercise eases symptoms." 2017.

Now that I had a workout plan and schedule, I needed a motivating playlist to keep my spirits as positive as possible, so I chose a variety of upbeat songs. My favorite was a live version of a salsa hit performed by a popular artist. But although the music made me want to dance, the sadness made my feet feel like cement. Instead, I played my favorite song on repeat, envisioning myself dancing in the days after my testimony as a way to release the stale, heavy energy from my body and to celebrate the completion. Even with progress, I had a long way to go until I could have a celebratory dance.

Had I gone to a medical doctor during the time I was preparing my testimony, I am confident that he or she would have told me that my adrenaline and cortisol levels were dangerously elevated. My fight or flight response had been activated since the day I received that letter. Regular exercise and meditation had reduced it, thankfully. However, my anxiety had become more intense during the moments when I physically sat down to type my speech. The testimony preparation process had stirred feelings that I thought I had examined, resolved, and neatly packed away years ago. Of all the feelings I felt, anger was most palpable, even this long after my brother's death. I was still angry that someone fired a loaded semi-automatic weapon at my brother as he ran away, angry that the convicted murderers were not sentenced to life, angry that people withheld kindness and compassion from Ma and me because they blamed my brother for his death, angry that homicide is an epidemic in my hometown and other urban centers in the United States, and angry that my son does not have an uncle. I was angry that this traumatic loss had caused irreparable damage to my mother's heart, soul, and spirit. Had my mother allowed herself to feel into the depth of her pain, I surmised, it might have plunged her into a pool of grief so deep that recovery may have felt impossible.

I connected the dots and realized the source of my fight or flight response: I had been preparing for the Parole Board panel as if I were preparing for a fight. My instinct to fight *for* my brother was valid and understandable. Against whom (or what) was I fighting, though? My conscious mind knew that the Board members were not my adversaries. I wanted them to render a decision that I favored. For the sake of my mental and physical health and well-being, I needed to ground this anger constructively, otherwise, I might be consumed by it. I chose to move away from the feelings of fighting against anyone or anything, and instead, pour all that I could into creating and delivering a strong testimony.

By the end of July, I was pleased with my progress. My speech was not as complete as I wanted it to be; transitional sentences were missing here and there. However, I trusted that the right words would find me while I addressed the panel, so I emailed the final version of the slide deck to my advocate so that she could share a copy with the panel. After the foundation of the speech had been completed, I decided to switch gears and start to internalize my testimony, as I wanted to deliver it as effortlessly as possible. Talking about my brother had always brought me to tears, and it was important for me to find ways to manage the tears so that I could deliver my speech in the manner I imagined. It felt important to begin my testimony by stating the difficult, painful fact that my brother was ambushed by two people on a Philadelphia street. The ability to express this truth aloud without completely breaking down in tears felt like a marker on my healing journey. I recited the opening line over and over until I could do so without crying. I practiced my speech with determination—and with a box of facial tissue nearby.

In the spirit of ripping away the Band-Aid and putting an end to the anticipation, I selected the first appointment of the day. At 9:00 a.m. on Tuesday, August 14, 2018, I gave my testimony to the Parole Board panel. That morning, I was not surprised when I woke up well in advance of my alarm. I seldom sleep well in hotels, and my lack of restorative sleep was exacerbated by my long-term PTSD-induced disordered sleeping and the stress surrounding the Parole Board testimony. I felt sick. I sat on the bed, took a few deep breaths, and meditated. This was it; the day for which I had prepared. With only a few hours of sleep, I arrived in Harrisburg about two hours early and scored a parking spot on the street directly across from Strawberry Square, a mixed-use shopping mall located downtown. I sat in the rental car until the plaza opened. When it did, my first order of business was to locate the lavatory, in case my nausea progressed.

The building was virtually empty and silent, aside from the clicking of my shoes on the floors. I had a printed copy of the PowerPoint slides with notes written all over it, so I found a table in the corner of a deli/store and tried to sit still while glancing over them. I wasn't hungry, but I knew that having a light breakfast was wise. Too much food was an invitation for a stomachache, a lack of nourishment was an invitation for a headache. I needed fuel to get through the sixty-minute testimony, so I purchased a banana and water.

The clock ticked slowly, but eventually, it was time to make my way to the building. I drove to the nondescript office location, rode the small elevator upstairs, and met with my advocate, who provided an overview of what to expect. Then, she guided me to the small conference room where I met three others: the Hearing Examiner, one Parole Board member, and an OVA staff member who was recording my testimony to share with the other eight Parole Board members. Just as I practiced, I delivered my speech, and to my delight, it went well—better than I expected. Delivering all salient points to the members of the Parole Board felt like a step toward reclaiming my voice. A voice that was stifled when the bailiff barked at me to put my notebook away during trial nineteen years ago.

After giving my testimony, I chatted with the Hearing Examiner and Board member and thanked them for their time and consideration of my recommendations. The Board member inquired about my occupation, guessing either attorney or teacher. I laughed and told her that neither was correct. She continued, saying, "Either way, that's some schtick you've got there." Schtick. I had only heard that word used to describe a comedian's performance. Was that supposed to be a compliment? It didn't sound like it. Her response felt inappropriate. Perhaps I should not have been surprised; this Board member also thought it prudent to interject during my presentation to correct my word choice. I thought that I had heard it all, rude comments, intrusive questions, and distasteful jokes—until this moment. I compartmentalized my feelings and focused on the joy that I felt for having met my objective.

Just a few moments later, my advocate invited me to sit with her at a small roundtable just outside of the conference room. She asked how I was feeling and extended the use of an office if I wanted to gather myself before driving back to Philadelphia. After politely declining, she provided an overview of the next steps: within the next two weeks, the inmate will make his presentation to the panel, and the panel will decide to either grant or deny parole, at which point my advocate will call me to convey the decision. I thanked her for everything and made my way out of the building. I was pleased with my testimony. I felt so energized and ready to drive back to Philadelphia before catching my flight back to Texas.

Three weeks later, while I was at the gym, I received a call from a number that began with "717." I recognized it as a Harrisburg area code and immediately felt my stomach begin to churn from anxiety. It was my advocate calling to inform me that the Parole Board had rendered its decision: denial of the inmate's request for parole. He would be eligible to reapply to be paroled in eighteen months, meaning that the second round of the parole process could begin in twelve months. My testimony had influenced the Parole Board's decision, as did the inmate's history of violent behavior during the early years of his incarceration. I felt both accomplished and relieved about the decision, as if my voice really mattered. I believe that Ma would have also been pleased. All of the stress that I experienced during the prior three months was well worth this outcome.

Although this was great news, it also meant that I would need to prepare for another round of testimony sooner than I had anticipated. While I was mentally prepared, I also felt depleted, as I thought I had given everything in my first testimony. I began to think about what I would say during the next one.

In October 2019, I received a familiar-looking envelope from Pennsylvania's Office of the Victim Advocate. As before, I called the number listed in the letter and scheduled my second testimony for the first inmate: Thursday, January 16, 2020. Unlike the first time, I was unable to travel to Harrisburg, so we agreed to conduct the testimony via teleconference. While thinking about my central theme for the presentation, the unsavory experience of having had my presentation referred to as a schtick returned to my memory. I was furious all over again.

Much like the initial touchpoint from my first assigned OVA advocate, I tried to shake off my hurt feelings so that I could focus on preparing my testimony for the second Parole Board panel. Preparation for my first Parole Board testimony took me to a dark place and having my presentation referred to as a schtick was reductive, belittling, and insensitive. It had left a scar. I offered this feedback to my advocate who confirmed this Board member's reputation as being insensitive and reassured me that she would not be in attendance at my upcoming Parole Board presentation. This was good news for me, yet I wondered how many homicide survivors had been subjected to her rudeness.

Between 2018 and 2022, I made a total of four presentations to the Pennsylvania Board of Parole, two for each co-defendant. The retrospective examination that began in 2018 had not stopped. With each testimony, I felt increasingly comfortable leaning into painful experiences so that I might connect the traumatic loss to my behavioral reactions. Preparation for each was a difficult emotional endeavor. The repetitive nature of this task did not make it easier; I needed just as much emotional support preparing for the fourth presentation as I did for the first.

The Parole Board process has ended.

Both inmates have been released.

A Hopeful Spring

1. What has your relationship with time been like since the loss of your loved one?

2. In what ways have you been expressing your grief?

3. What activities did you enjoy before the loss of your loved one? How often have you engaged in those since the loss of your loved one?

4. Are you familiar with survivor's guilt? If so, do you think you are experiencing it?

5. Can you name the feelings that you have or have had since the loss of your loved one? How has each impacted you? How are you constructively managing the negative feelings?

6. Are you comfortable asking for support? If not, what impacts your willingness to ask others for help or support?

7. Who are the members of your support team? Are you spending enough time with each?

8. What have been your experiences with therapists and/or grief counselors?

9. What has been your experience with organizations whose objective is to support homicide survivors?

10. What has been your experience with the criminal justice system and its representatives?

REFLECTIONS:

PART III

It's Complicated

CHAPTER SIX

Movies, Music, and Language

After much reflection and clarity, I realized that I have developed complicated relationships with people, places, and things in response to my brother's murder. During my early years of grief, I attended a support group meeting for homicide survivors and heard a participant use the word "anniversary" when referring to the date of her loved one's death. It struck me as odd, and I'm sure that my facial expression conveyed that. In my experience, an anniversary was a positive occasion worth celebrating. I don't want to celebrate the date that my brother was murdered. However, as I went on to learn, Webster defines an anniversary as the annual occurrence of a date marking a notable event.[23] The definition does not actually indicate that the event has to be positive, and the date of my brother's death was certainly notable, as it marked the day that my life changed forever.

Even though the word "anniversary" doesn't necessarily mean that the occasion being observed is cheerful, I met many survivors within that group who consciously engaged in activities or rituals on

---

23 "Anniversary Definition & Meaning."

the anniversary to offset the day's heavy emotions, like releasing balloons or visiting the cemetery to feel close to a deceased loved one. That support group was not the last time I heard survivors use the word, either. Before I knew it, I adopted "anniversary" to refer to the date that changed my life.

Until 1999, I had not noticed how normalized the use of violent phrases in everyday conversation had become. In Philadelphia, many people used an expression that was jarring to hear but still widely accepted. "I was so mad, I could have shot someone." After losing my brother, listening to violent language became problematic for me both in social settings and the workplace, as co-workers invited me to "shoot them an email" with details of upcoming events, to "do a drive-by" when describing a quick trip to someone's office or cubicle, or telling someone that they "killed it" as a way to convey a job well done. During the early years of grief, I was shocked by the extent to which violent language and phrases were casually used. This language existed years before my brother's murder, but growing up in places where violence is normalized can desensitize even the most sensitive person. After my brother's death, hearing these words and phrases became personal and intolerable. I could no longer remain desensitized.

Similarly, I have become painfully aware of how much gun violence exists in music and movies. Weeks after my brother's funeral, I was at a friend's place watching a sports-themed film where there were many scenes of hope and optimism along with light-hearted moments between family members. All was going well until a montage quickly appeared on the screen that included the image of a young man's hand squeezing the trigger of a handgun. The combination of that unexpected visual along with the sound of gunfire proved too much for me. I immediately jumped up from the couch and ran away from the television into another room and cried hysterically. This was a pivotal experience for me; that night, I realized that consuming images and sounds that either depicted gun violence or suggested homicide had the potential to cause a shift in my energy (I prefer to use this phrase instead of "trigger" because the latter reminds me of gun violence). So, I decided to change my viewing habits. After that night, I did my best to screen new films before watching them.

A few months later, I was listening to the radio while riding in the car with the same friend who had witnessed my movie meltdown. A song that was popular during our high school days began to play. Initially, we struggled to recall the words, but midway through the first verse, we found our rhythm and began singing along. That is, until we reached the second verse when I heard the lyric that referenced killing someone. I immediately stopped singing. To his credit, my friend caught it too, quickly changed the station, and tried to move us past that painful moment. However, no matter how hard I try, shielding myself from gun violence continues to be difficult, as it remains so pervasive in American culture.

In addition to language, I had become sensitive to death imagery. I noticed it everywhere. I remember driving in the Carolinas, seeing a dead animal along the shoulder of a country road and weeping in response. I remember experiencing expressions of emotion in the presence of others—both strangers and friends. In those instances, I felt embarrassed for having an emotional outburst around people who may neither be interested nor equipped to offer a constructive reaction to it. Expecting others to develop sensitivities and change behaviors overnight is both unrealistic and unfair. I did not want people to feel obligated to console me in response to a pain about which they likely knew nothing. I did not know how to articulate all of that, so I withdrew. I became reclusive (and perhaps boring to some) because solitude had become a safe space.

I developed a process to vet and onboard people whom I met socially. Protecting myself from harsh images and unsafe surroundings was critical, and I felt compelled to convey that. I talked about activities that I did not enjoy: watching movies with gun violence, watching the local news, listening to violent music, being surprised, playing laser tag/paintball/with water guns, and hearing fireworks. Any activity that simulated mortally wounding another with a gun of any sort was off-limits for me. The list of things that offended me was longer than the list of things in which I found joy.

It wasn't until 2018 that I could find the words to express the impact that my brother's death had on me in one simple sentence: I had become fearful of the world. With my brother around, I always felt safe, but during my first few trips to Philadelphia following his death, the city felt different. I remember walking to the mailbox just a few short blocks away from Ma's house and being consumed with an unsettling feeling. I looked over my shoulder every few seconds as if to check whether someone was suspiciously walking behind me. That crime existed was no secret, but the specter of crime now loomed so large that walking to the nearby mailbox made me feel uneasy.

During the first year, I called my mother regularly, but one week, I was feeling depressed and unsure that I could mask it from her, so I didn't call home. A couple of days later, I returned home from work and saw that the red light on my answering machine was blinking, indicating the presence of a new unheard message. I pressed "Play." It was Ma, saying hello and casually expressing concern because she had not heard from me. Although her message was controlled, I could hear the worry in her voice. The last time she did not hear from her child as expected, the reason was grave. In that moment of listening to the tone of her voice, I recognized that she carried a fear for my safety that ran much deeper than anything I could imagine. I had not fully appreciated how her voice message impacted me until years later. It was not until Parole Board preparation that I realized the extent to which, in some respects, I had tip-toed through life so as not to cause her any worry.

My fear was debilitating and controlling. It was a persuasive liar and thief, whispering in my ear that the harm accompanying exploration exceeded the reward it promised. It urged me to follow the path laden with experiences that guaranteed safety. While it may have served a well-intended purpose during the first few years of grief, this fear stayed well beyond its welcome.

CHAPTER SEVEN

Transparency, Time, and My Hometown

I n my early years of grief, meeting new people had the potential to be stressful and anxiety-inducing for one reason: it challenged my relationship with transparency. In an attempt to get to know you, strangers tend to inquire about your family background during small talk. Though I had withdrawn from many gatherings, there were occasions I could not avoid that required me to socialize with new people. I would do my best to steer the conversation away from myself, and although it worked for a while, the conversation around my family would come up ... every single time.

For unknown reasons, many people assumed that I had no siblings, even going as far as to say, "I can tell that you're an only child." In those early years, I felt like I was dishonoring my brother by denying his existence, so I would correct them by saying that I grew up with a brother. This often led to a barrage of questions about him, like, "How old is he? What does he do?"

I would reply by stating, "He was older than me, but he passed away," hoping that it would end this line of questioning. But often, awkwardness followed, and I found myself either having to console the listener who could never imagine losing a sibling or having to field the question that I dread most: *What happened?* The first couple of times, I answered this question truthfully but quickly learned how much of a mistake that was. Too often, I left these exchanges feeling exposed and empty. Talking about my brother stirred up sad feelings, and the listener was either uninterested or oblivious to it.

I recall sharing a moment of transparency with a person in a leadership position where I was employed. After hearing that my brother was murdered, she expressed sadness that my mother lost a son. The atrocity of murder did not seem to bother her. Rather, she lamented the loss of my mother's male child. Her response left me deflated, offended, and horrified.

It took me some time to realize that I did not owe anyone information that I deemed personal. I learned that people's curiosity and entitlement will lead them to ask questions that are, frankly, none of their business, so the responsibility rested with me to be prepared and respond accordingly. I gave myself permission to withhold details about my brother and answer questions only if I wanted to. I reframed my silence as a protective act, one that neither dishonored his memory nor denied his existence. For the situations where I preferred not to answer people's questions, I would brainstorm anticipated questions, wordsmith, and memorize one or two responses. Over time, I built an inventory of responses that I could easily tap into, based on the context, questions, and audience. (Have I mentioned how exhausting being a survivor has been?!)

My relationship with time and its function throughout my grief journey porpoised like an embattled boat in a storm. During the early months of grief, I leaned on time, wishing to propel it forward so that I could follow. I wanted the days to advance quickly to fast-forward through the intense pain. I wanted time to pull me out of my sadness. However, I believe that my healing process would have been better served by giving myself time to slowly settle into the reality of my brother's homicide by facing the pain, as unbearable as it was. I needed to fall apart just enough to acknowledge and embrace the fact that I was not okay. I needed time to breathe, to feel, and to start the process of coming to terms with this traumatic loss without rushing to feign normalcy. I simply needed time to put the pieces back together.

After two decades, I have realized that the pain neither diminishes nor disappears and that I was waiting for permission to cry and feel neither bad nor embarrassed about it. I wanted to be freed from the notion that a prescribed timeline would cure my broken heart. Usually, when anything brought my emotions to the surface, whether in company or alone, I would berate myself, stating over and over again that I should be okay after the amount of time that had passed. But now, after practicing self-care and facing my grief head-on, I learned to welcome the emotions—reminding myself that the tears are only a sign of my love for my brother.

One night, while writing this book, I washed, rolled my hair, and sat under the hooded dryer. It takes close to two hours for my hair to dry, which is ideal for movie-watching. I selected a comedy that centered around the upheaval that ensued after two men mysteriously swapped lives. One of the last scenes of the film was a banquet-style award dinner honoring one of the main characters. The co-star stood at the podium and introduced the award recipient, beginning with his name, hometown, and full birthday. I was shocked to hear the date; it was my brother's birthday. Tears welled up in my eyes. I no longer shame myself for having these human reactions, so I leaned into them at that moment, allowing myself to reflect on how special my brother is to me and all the moments that bring his memory to life.

Perhaps the most notable complicated relationship that developed is the one with my hometown. I remember returning to Philadelphia for winter break during my college freshman year. It was evening, and I was washing my hands in the bathroom. I heard the front door open, followed by heavy footsteps landing on the hardwood floors. "Where is she?" he asked Ma.

"Upstairs," I heard her say.

In what felt like seconds, Keith opened the bathroom door without knocking and said, "Kim!" and hugged me. I marveled at his face, which now sported a full beard. It was so good to see him. The pain becomes unbearable when I think about how I will never see his face, hear his voice, or be greeted like that again.

Keith and I attended the same school until the end of middle school. For the most part, teachers, staff, and students from our elementary and middle schools could identify all students and their siblings. So, while I was back in Philadelphia for trial during the summer of 1999 and was running some errands with friends, I heard a voice call my name from inside one of the stores we were walking past. I turned my head to see one of my classmates wearing a big smile on his face. We chatted for a few moments before he asked, "How's Keith?" I told my classmate what happened and he naturally extended his condolences. Then, we exchanged awkward goodbyes.

The next stop my friends and I made was our alma mater. Per protocol, we stopped at the guardhouse at the campus entrance and were greeted by a well-tenured guard who remembered every student, sibling, and parent. He asked how Keith and Ma were doing. As I did with my classmate, I responded with honesty. With a look of terror, he expressed how shocked he was and extended his regrets. How does one end a conversation after it takes such an awful turn? I held it together during both conversations, but I felt exhausted by the end of that day.

Every spring, my alma mater welcomes alumni and their families back to campus for what can best be described as homecoming. As much as I wanted to visit in 2000, I knew that I would be asked the same question multiple times while walking the campus—not to mention, the awkwardness that would follow my response. So, I chose not to attend. Over the past twenty-plus years, each spring, I prepared what I thought was a compelling pep talk to myself, "Next year, I'll go back." But my pep talks proved no match for my desire to avoid anxiety and discomfort. With each passing year, it became more difficult to return to my hometown for extended periods. Reconnecting to an ecosystem that was vital during my youth seemed no longer possible. It felt as if I missed my window.

I was appreciative of the fact that I lived away from my hometown after Keith's passing, as it afforded me the space to wrap my mind around the loss and the chance to heal away from the place where the loss happened. Having this distance was helpful while I navigated the healing journey during my early years of grief. However, when I wanted to reconnect with familiar people and places, the distance felt like a hurdle. A few months after beginning to write this book, it suddenly felt as if my worries had been heard as I reconnected with a classmate to whom I had not spoken in ten years. We caught up and had some frank discussions about many things—including the reasons for my distance. He reassured me that the community would welcome me back with understanding and since then, I have had other opportunities to reconnect with classmates and old friends who have not only said but shown me the same thing. These reconnections and closing the distance have been so healing.

CHAPTER EIGHT

By and By

To say that I had a strong faith foundation before my brother's murder would be untrue. After my parents divorced, Ma, Keith, and I left New Jersey and returned to Philadelphia. Ma worked multiple jobs so she could provide for us and had two babysitters for Keith and me—one for the weekdays and another for the weekends.

Our babysitters lived around the corner from one another and attended the same church. I remember attending worship service with them for a short while, always sitting in a pew with the rest of the family members for service. I enjoyed listening to the choir and was amazed when the adults shouted as a way to show their praise.

A couple of years later, I began attending a church with my father on the weekends during which I was in his care. The church was within walking distance of the housing projects where my father lived with his girlfriend. For reasons not fully known to me (although, I have a guess), I was not given my father's last name, which was Combs. On our first visit to this church, he and I stood during the portion of the service when visitors were invited to introduce themselves. As we stood and waited for our turn to speak, my father leaned down to get closer to my ear and instructed me to lie about my name. "Introduce yourself as Kimberly Combs," he said. I was uncomfortable but agreed. I was about nine years old, so did I have a choice? Eventually, we joined the church, and I continued to attend with him under this pseudonym.

My father's motivation for church attendance likely centered around keeping up appearances in a way that benefited him. I include the words "in a way that benefited him" with confidence. During my lifetime, he has only done things that offered him an advantage of some kind, reduced his financial obligation, or let him pass the buck on his parental responsibility.

During our tenure as church members, there was little focus on my spiritual development. When I was not serving as an usher, I sat in service with the adults and doodled on the church program. Church attendance was paramount. However, neither the principles of the religious text nor the importance of developing a relationship with God was stressed. The person taking me to church lacked such a relationship, so he was ill-equipped to champion my spiritual development. Superficial and fraught with problems, this early church experience was my introduction to recurring themes related to integrity, compassion, and honesty that seemed to resurface throughout my experiences with institutions of organized religion. Then, as an adult, Ma's and my experiences with church leaders who failed to offer pastoral care only served as more evidence that homicide survivors were often left to fend for themselves.

Shortly after my brother's death, random people began to talk about forgiveness—rather, my need to forgive the murderers—as an integral part of the healing process. Those people were neither emotionally close to me nor knowledgeable about the impact that homicide has on surviving loved ones, and none of them expressed sincere interest in whether I was healing holistically. Their focus was singular; convincing me to forgive. Most of the people who advocated forgiveness were self-described Bible-following Christians, which did not come as a surprise since I was living in the Bible Belt. I was advised that forgiveness was for me, not the murderers. Although I had no intention of forgiving, my curiosity got the best of me and led me to ask: how does one forgive murderers? What are the steps?

According to them, saying "I forgive <insert murderer's name here>" was the first step in the process of forgiving. The advice was predicated on the notion that a declaration of forgiveness would pierce my hardened heart and initiate a healing transformation. This action would supposedly lead to harmony between those words and feelings of belief. Had I uttered those words, it would have been a performative lie. It would have also meant that I succumbed to the pressure to placate others. When I was a child asked to lie about my name to church leaders and members, I had no choice. As an adult, I have agency, and self-betrayal in the name of forgiveness of my brother's murderers is an offense that I am unwilling to commit. In no way am I belittling anyone's belief that forgiveness is possible. I firmly believe that the process of forgiveness begins when the survivor is organically ready. And I was not.

While others were pressuring me to forgive, my mind remained fixed on the existential themes that bubbled up immediately after my brother's murder. On the morning of the funeral, I awoke with an intense feeling of dread and cried throughout the morning while getting dressed. After using an inordinate amount of facial tissue, I decided to use something more sustainable to catch my tears. In addition to clothing, I packed my favorite set of towels, which were orange, and included bath and hand towels and one washcloth. Orange was such a vibrant color that typically lifted my mood, and while I knew that no amount of color could lighten the heaviness of this day, I was desperate to try. I grabbed my orange hand towel and held it as we piled into the limousine for the quiet ride to the funeral. During the funeral, Ma and I sat on the front pew of the small country church. I sat leaning forward almost touching my lap, crying with my face in my hands. With her left arm, Ma pulled me close to her.

During the funeral, I sat up to watch and listen as others sang hymns of praise. The last line of the refrain from a particular hymn has been etched into my memory ever since. It references someone being happy. On one of the saddest days of my life, there was no way that I could sing about feeling happy. I did not understand how the pain of a murdered loved one and mourners' expressions of love for Christ coexisted at this moment. The louder they sang, the louder I cried into my tear-soaked towel. What was more alarming to me was that Ma was one of those people singing, with tears rolling down the left side of her face. Praising anything or anyone was the furthest from my mind. Instead, I wanted to know why God let my brother die. A God that protects would not have allowed this to happen, I reasoned. Why did He let my brother die? Didn't God know that letting my brother die would wreck my mom and me?

Those early experiences with organized religion and religious people left an indelible impression on me. After 1999, I wanted nothing to do with people who professed to be believers of Christ. When someone recited scriptures to me, I either tuned them out or politely found ways to terminate the conversation. My encounters with a member of the homicide survivors support group in North Carolina were pivotal in my spiritual development. During a meeting, a couple of us recounted how people of faith immediately responded to us following our loved ones' deaths. I talked about the pastor's refusal to host my brother's funeral, and another woman told us about the day that she found a Bible verse taped to her door, one that stressed the importance of repenting for our sins. Both responses were rooted in victim-blaming and shaming.

As a Christian woman, the group member I mentioned above was mortified to hear our stories and was eager to offer both of us a better experience. She invited us to attend church with her and, eventually, I agreed. I'm glad that I did; I had a delightful time. I enjoyed the teaching and was gifted with a Bible. I was encouraged to read it and begin to discover Christ for myself instead of relying on the examples set by others. Specific scriptures were emphasized for my study, as they might offer comfort while grieving. Shortly after that church visit, I moved to Texas, and I never returned to that church in North Carolina. Even so, that experience reminded me to resist the urge to stereotype everyone who professed to be a believer in a certain faith. But before I reengaged with organized religion, I knew that it was imperative to somehow extend it a fresh start and vow to evaluate people based on their merit.

After my relocation to Texas, I continued to read that Bible, and after some convincing by a co-worker, I began attending Bible study, then Sunday service. Roughly five years after my brother's funeral, I was attending service regularly. On one of the Sundays, as instructed by the minister, I picked up the hymnal from the pew in front of me and turned to the requested page. Many congregants were familiar with the lyrics, needing only to occasionally glance at the hymnal. As one of the newer members without much knowledge of the classic hymns, I buried my nose in the hymnal so that I could follow. The melody was familiar but without having time to think of where I heard it before, I just followed along and continued to sing. When I reached the end of the first verse, I recognized the refrain and stopped singing before hearing the verse in which the hymn writer sang about being happy.

A well-known hymn whose refrain may be more recognizable than its title, "Alas! And Did My Savior Bleed" is theologically rich and important to many Christians. The hymn represents Christ's agape love for humankind, faith, hope, and redemption through propitiation.[24] At that moment, as I started singing again, all I could think about was the sorrow I felt when I heard these words during my brother's funeral. I was unable to connect to the hymn's messages despite my earnest desire to do so.

My existential crisis persisted during the first few years after my brother's murder, leading to stress and wasted energy. I felt myself beginning to spiral down a dark path that led nowhere. I would never get satisfactory answers. Eventually, my emotional exhaustion led me to surrender, and I stopped asking why. As I developed spiritually, my perspective shifted, and I began to understand why some mourners sing hymns of praise during funerals. I embraced the notion that I was meant to live a life full of joy despite having experienced this traumatic loss. I accepted that this experience of deep loss was mine to carry and held tightly to the idea that, while I may not have an answer to my "why" question, in the fullness of time, I would develop the competencies that I needed to navigate this loss.

24 Hudson, 2022.

It's Complicated

1. Have you developed sensitivity to language?

2. Are there any rituals that you have created to observe the anniversary of the loss of your loved one?

3. Have you noticed a difference in the kind of music or movies that you enjoy watching?

4. Have you become sensitive to anything else since the loss of your loved one?

5. Have your sensitivities changed how you engage with others, either socially or professionally?

6. Have you communicated those sensitivities to others in either your personal or professional networks?

7. Do you often feel afraid? How has that fear impacted your decision-making?

8. Are you carrying someone else's fear?

9. Has the lens through which you view the world changed? If you view it in negative terms, do you want to change that?

10. Have you withdrawn from familiar people and places? How has that helped?

11. Have you found that others have withdrawn from you since the loss?

12. What is your comfort level with interacting with strangers?

13. How comfortable are you with talking about your loved one with strangers? Co-workers?

14. Have you felt pressured to forgive the person/people responsible for your loved one's murder?

15. Have you felt pressured to conform to a certain faith's practice as part of your healing journey?

16. How have you been able to draw upon your faith during the healing journey?

17. Have you questioned your faith during this time?

18. How has your faith changed since the loss of your loved one?

19. What messages have you heard about the role of time in the healing process? Do the messages resonate with you?

20. Have you created any rituals, habits, or practices that have eased your grief?

21. Has your concept of home changed since the death of your loved one?

22. Do you live in the same city or town where your loved one was murdered? If so, have you modified how you navigate through the city or town?

REFLECTIONS:

CHAPTER NINE

Conclusion

A not-so-simple question placed me squarely on my healing journey nineteen years after my brother's death. The questions printed in the written material produced by the Pennsylvania Board of Parole dwarfed the surrounding text, inviting me to answer the following: what continuing effects have the crime had on me? My visceral responses to this question were a quiet scoff and a dismissive head shake. The answer was obvious: my brother's murder ruined everything.

After some reflection, I realized that my reaction was not directed at the question itself, but instead, it was a response from the part of me that found comfort in staying on the surface and using superlatives, like, "Losing my brother is the worst thing that happened to me." These responses were substitutes for language that I had never developed. Not once during the past nineteen years had I tried to articulate the wreckage that had become my mental and emotional states after my brother's homicide. Little did I know, that was about to change.

In retrospect, answering this question was a gift. It was an invitation for me to intentionally reflect on how my brother's murder had affected me immediately following the loss in 1999 and during the years that followed. Given their professional experiences, Parole Board members know that homicide creates irreparable damage for surviving loved ones. I had an invitation to spend sixty minutes sharing an honest and raw account of my thoughts, feelings, and experiences, and I leaned into it, creating the moment that began a life shift for me.

The revelations that resulted from my examination of the impacts of my brother's homicide were pivotal. Giving testimony to the Pennsylvania Board of Parole presented an opportunity for me to sit with this question. Had a therapist asked me this question, I am certain that I would have found a way to half-heartedly complete the exercise. But anything less than a sincere effort would have been a disservice to me; I would have robbed myself of the chance for meaningful self-exploration. For reasons previously mentioned, being asked this question by the Parole Board was different—my participation was required and had a material impact on parole outcomes. Parole Board panel testimony was the impetus for my taking an active role in finding some semblance of the joy that existed before that traumatizing loss.

When you feel compelled, I invite you to answer the following questions with radical honesty: how has your loved one's homicide affected you? What are the continuing effects of this loss?

"Nobody cares." I can hear Ma's voice so clearly telling me that. Despite having had many unsavory experiences throughout my grief journey, I know that people do in fact care. Across the United States, several individuals and organizations are engaged in important work to reduce the tentacles of gun violence and homicide. Some provide advocacy services and support to families of homicide victims. Others focus on public policy, socio-economic factors, or behavioral themes related to power and strength, anger management, and healthy conflict resolution to reduce homicide and gun violence. There is no shortage of work to do related to prospective and retrospective examinations of the impacts of homicide. I encourage survivors to center their healing and be introspective to listen for internal nudges.

If you feel compelled, consider either working independently or volunteering with organizations that seek to address the perils of gun violence. Some survivors may feel led to support restorative justice efforts or examine linkages between cultures of silence and cooperation with the criminal justice system. Others might feel inspired to volunteer with coalitions working to solve cold cases. As naive as it sounds, I believe that homicide survivors are uniquely positioned to positively impact this work and make meaningful changes in the world. I just wish that Ma could have lived long enough to have participated in it.

My brother's homicide changed me on a cellular level. The version of myself that existed before January 1999 is gone, and I will not pretend that I am the same. However, I choose to find the color in this version of my existence, one that feels surreal at times. I find myself occupying various positions on a spectrum between the extremes of stillness and movement, mourning and celebrating, death and life. But even when death is all around, life exists. I have permitted myself to enjoy life without guilt. I choose to continue moving toward healing.

I choose to see life in color.

If There is a Homicide Survivor in Your Life:

Homicide survivors are not monolithic, and offering emotional support to a survivor of trauma is not always easy. It requires patience and grace, as our emotions and moods may fluctuate from merry to melancholy in a matter of hours. Our expressions of grief might challenge your notions of what the grieving process should look like. If you're unsure where to begin, consider asking the survivor in your life, "How can I help?" You may receive an answer that expresses uncertainty, which is to be expected given the complexity and gravity of both the grief and the circumstances. Ask this question often, as their needs may change over time. In hindsight, I wish my friends and extended family would have offered to listen to my Parole Board testimonies. I would have welcomed an honest, "I don't know what to say," followed by an embrace. Offering a listening ear, extending an invitation to binge-watch movies, or having a virtual chat session can do wonders for the homicide survivor in your life.

Whiskey Tango Foxtrot

By Kimberly Christopher (November 2021)

Just read the news, and it breaks my heart—it's up to 500 again.
The homicide rate is appalling and maddening. I don't know if it will ever end.

Arguments, affronts, or feeling disrespected
The ego's response? A round of gunfire
Feel better? You can't. In no way was that necessary
This destructive way of coping we should retire.

In the early 90s, I read an article in which the author said it was twenty-five;
the life expectancy of a black man in America.
I thought, "This guy's an alarmist. This can't be true."
If I knew then what I know now, his theory I would not deride.

Is it a public health problem? Or do we examine the home?
Maybe the family unit is to blame
Year after year the City reeks of apathy and feels heavy with inaction
And that is the real shame.

Generations snuffed out in an instant
Wives mourning husbands and moms mourning sons
Can we ever sever this conflict resolution tactic of using life-ending guns?

Whiskey tango foxtrot are we going to do?
Why can't we band together and rise above?
When will you start to live up to your moniker, my dear City of Brotherly
Love?

Acknowledgments

My grief journey has been a long and winding road, and I am fortunate to have had support along the way. Some people arrived at the right time and stayed only for a moment; others have been here for years. Whether you met Ma and me at the courthouse for the hearings, offered kindness in words or deeds, empathized with me during my bouts of insomnia, showed genuine interest in Parole Board outcomes, or just held space for me to cry, I want to express my gratitude to you. I appreciate you deeply.

Appendix

1. "Criminal Justice Process - Office of the District Attorney: City of Philadelphia." n.d. Philadelphia District Attorney's Office. Accessed March 22, 2024. https://phillyda.org/safety-and-justice/criminal-justice-process/.

2. IBID

3. "Philadelphia Preliminary Hearing Lawyer | Preliminary Hearing Attorney in Pennsylvania." n.d. Lento Law Firm. Accessed March 22, 2024. https://www.josephlento.com/criminal-process/preliminary-hearings.

4. IBID

5. "234 Pa. Code Rule 590. Pleas and Plea Agreements." n.d. Pennsylvania Bulletin. Accessed March 22, 2024. https://www.pacodeandbulletin.gov/Display/pacode?file=/secure/pacode/data/234/chapter5/s590.html&d=reduce.

6. IBID

7. "Parole 101." n.d. PA Parole Board. Accessed March 22, 2024. https://www.parole.pa.gov/Parole%20101/Pages/default.aspx.

8. IBID

9. IBID

10. "Parole Interview." n.d. PA Parole Board. Accessed March 22, 2024. https://www.parole.pa.gov/Parole%20Process/Parole%20Interview/Pages/default.aspx.

11. "Decision Makers - Parole Process." n.d. PA.Gov. Accessed March 22, 2024. https://www.parole.pa.gov/Parole%20Process/Decision%20Makers/Pages/default.aspx.

12. IBID

13. "The Pennsylvania Parole Process." n.d. Pennsylvania Department of Corrections. Accessed March 22, 2024. https://www.parole.pa.gov/

Parole%20101/Documents/Parole%20101/FINAL%20Parole%20
Process%20FLOWCHART.pdf.

14. "Homicide Victims/Co-Survivors | Office for Victims of Crime."
    2020. Office for Victims of Crime. https://ovc.ojp.gov/topics/
    homicide-victims-co-survivors.

15. IBID.

16. Green BL. Traumatic loss: Conceptual and empirical links between
    trauma and bereavement. *Journal of Personal and Interpersonal
    Loss.* 2000;5:1–17

17. Green BL, Krupnick JL, Stockton P, Goodman L, Corcoran C, Petty R.
    Psychological outcomes associated with traumatic loss in a sample of
    young women. *American Behavioral Scientist.* 2001;44:817–837.

18. Rynearson Edward K., McCreery JM. *Bereavement after homicide: a syn-
    ergism of trauma and loss.* Am J Psychiatry. 1993 Feb;150(2):258-61. doi:
    10.1176/ajp.150.2.258. PMID: 8422076.

19. McDevitt-Murphy, Meghan E., Neimeyer, Robert A., Burke,
    Laurie A., Williams, Joah A., & Lawson, Katherine (2012).
    The Toll of Traumatic Loss in African Americans Bereaved
    by Homicide. *Psychological Trauma: Theory, Research, Practice, and
    Policy, 4*(3), 303–311. https://doi.org/10.1037/a0024911

20. Zinzow, Heidi, Rheingold Alyssa A., Hawkins Alesia, Saunders Benjamin,
    Kilpatrick Dean G. Losing a loved one to homicide: prevalence and
    mental health correlates in a national sample of young adults. J Trauma
    Stress. 2009 Feb;22(1):20-7. doi: 10.1002/jts.20377. PMID: 19230006;
    PMCID: PMC2829865.

21. IBID.

22. "Depression and anxiety: Exercise eases symptoms." 2017. Mayo Clinic.
    https://www.mayoclinic.org/diseases-conditions/depression/in-depth/
    depression-and-exercise/art-20046495.

23. "Anniversary Definition & Meaning." n.d. Merriam-Webster. Accessed
    March 22, 2024. https://www.merriam-webster.com/dictionary/
    anniversary.

24. Hudson, Ralph F. 2022. "The Inspiring Message of "Alas, and Did My
    Savior Bleed."" iBelieve.com. https://www.ibelieve.com/faith/the-inspir-
    ing-message-of-alas-and-did-my-savior-bleed.html.

About the Author

Kimberly Christopher is a human resource practitioner who is passionate about advocacy and healing for homicide survivors. She is a member of the National Organization for Victim Advocacy. Even two decades after her brother's homicide, Kimberly's grief journey continues.

www.ingramcontent.com/pod-product-compliance
Lightning Source LLC
Chambersburg PA
CBHW051214120626
46547CB00013B/1347